NEIL GAUGHT

C⊙RE

THE SINGLE ORGANIZING IDEA
PLAYBOOK

The complete SOI® toolkit, including over 40 detailed diagrams and step-by-step explanations you can follow immediately to change your business for good

With a foreword by Julian Richer

Entrepreneur, philanthropist and author

SINGLE OR⊙
(S

PRAISE FOR CORE

'CORE: The Playbook is a breakthrough practical guide that global business leaders will use to become the vanguards for the world we want. And I fully expect it will become a critical resource for schools educating the global managers of today and the future.' Dr. Sanjeev Khagram, Dean & Director General, Professor of Global Leadership Thunderbird School of Global Management, University of Arizona

'The SOI® toolkit is a way that businesses can embark on a journey toward mutual prosperity that is both simple and scalable. Now, more than ever, solutions that encompass the need for sustainable and ethical business are key – the SOI® is such a solution.' Rajiv Joshi, Former MD of The B Team

'21st-century problems need powerful and practical 21st-century solutions to escalate progress, and Single Organizing Idea is one of them.' James Wallis, Co-founder of IBM Blockchain

'CORE: The Playbook is just how a book ought to be in the 2020s: short, accessible, original and full of clear practical guidance that enables companies to make the radical but necessary changes that the planet and people urgently need. For anyone who's starting to feel that the new corporate agenda is too much talk and not enough action, this is the remedy.' Simon Anholt, Policy advisor and researcher

'As we enter a decisive decade companies need to shift from ambition to action. The CORE Playbook is a practical guide for businesses to do just that.' Ben Kellard, Director of business strategy, the Cambridge Institute for Sustainability Leadership (CISL)

'Finally, a practical guide that not only shows you how to put purpose at the core of your business, but also provides the measurement tools to prove you're delivering sustainable prosperity for all.' Chip Conley, *New York Times* bestselling author, strategist and entrepreneur

'The SOI® uses a structured methodology that helps teams hold the core purpose central to all their actions, relationships and communications. B Corps, and any organization that is serious about being led by their purpose to do more than just seek profit, could be helped by this book.' Katie Hill, Executive Chair, B Lab Europe

'There's an urgent need for tools to help small and medium sized business to pivot and change for good, and here is a practical resource to help them do just that.' Nigel Topping, High Level Climate Action Champion, UNFCCC COP26

'An essential guide to building a 21st-century business where everyone feels great about contributing to a more meaningful and sustainable future.' Patrick Grant, celebrity fashion designer and founder of Community Clothing

'The most important lesson I have learned from my 50+ years of working with organizations on their values and culture is the necessity for a comprehensive cut-through accountability mechanism that supports the embodied living of values and the behaviours that demonstrate them. In CORE: The Playbook, for the first time, we have an approach and a tool with that power.' Gunther M Weil, Ph.D., Co-Founder & CEO of Value Mentors

For HALODI

First published 2020
by Renegade Assembly
Westwood Lodge, Saffron Walden, Essex CB10 2XT

British Library Cataloguing-in-Publication Data
A catalogue record for this book is available from the British Library

Library of Congress Cataloging-in-Publication Data
978-1-8382345-2-2 - .epub
978-1-8382345-3-9 - .mobi

Typeset in Futura

To Jane

Best wishes

Nevi.

FOREWORD

It's always seemed common sense to me that any business will be more successful in the long run if managed ethically and with due consideration for both economic and social return.

Access the
SOI® website

In May 2019 *The Guardian*, *The Times* and *The Financial Times* all wrote leader articles about my decision to transfer control of my business, Richer Sounds, to colleagues via an employee ownership trust à la John Lewis. I opened my first shop aged 19 and still really care about what we do and how we do it. But after 40 years of sole ownership, I was increasingly feeling the need to pass it on to the next generation and the pull to spend more time on my philanthropic projects.

It's a sad reality that this transition was deemed newsworthy simply because it remains highly unusual. Most owners in my position would have succumbed to the temptation to maximise personal gain as far as possible, with little regard for wider stakeholder interests.

It's always seemed common sense to me that any business will be more successful in the long run if it is managed ethically and with due consideration for both economic and social return.

Unsurprisingly, this is obvious to the general public too. A 2017 survey by Ipos Mori revealed that:

- Just 18% of consumers agreed the current economic system is working well for them and less than a third believe it is working well for businesses.
- Almost half of consumers (47%) believed that ethically run businesses are better for the economy and almost exactly the same proportion (48%) preferred to use or purchase from businesses that act ethically.
- 37% believed businesses should put social purpose ahead of making profits.
- 70% were more likely to purchase products or services from businesses paying employees a fair wage, and 47% were more likely to do the same for businesses which have a positive stance on social issues.
- 49% said they would not take a job with a business they believed to have behaved unethically.

In a separate survey run by Christian Aid the same year, 89% said that tax avoidance is morally wrong. That's before anyone had ever heard of Greta Thunberg, when *Blue Planet* was just a BBC nature program and not the catalyst for shoppers to leave plastic packaging in supermarket aisles, when Extinction Rebellion hadn't been born, 125 million kids weren't regularly going on climate strike, Kate Raworth's *Donut Economics* and my own book *The Ethical Capitalist* hadn't been added to the growing pile of books proposing a reboot of a kinder form of capitalism, and BlackRock's Larry Fink hadn't put the world's biggest corporations on notice to change – or else!

The good news is that there's an ever-increasing realisation in the business world that things have to change, and quickly. COVID-19 has brought into sharp focus that things are not working as they should and the media is full of stories about the need to change.

But change isn't easy and what we need is urgent change. For some time now, it's

frustrated me that there's an awful lot of theories and misleading fluff being written about purpose but very little of substance that shows how a business with a social purpose can make a difference. There are no tools, nor a systematic way to go about repurposing a business, and certainly very little for SMEs that lack the funds to employ expensive, salaried management consultants with no skin in the game.

Neil's Single Organizing Idea (SOI®) is a praiseworthy effort to address these barriers. A complete toolkit of diagrams and templates to help any business define, align and measure their SOI®, Neil's beautifully presented Playbook gives away everything he's learnt in 15 years of deploying the SOI® system around the world so that any business can make a start and, more importantly, see through change that sticks.

Why such generosity? Because he feels more than ever it's the right thing to do.

I applaud Neil's endeavour and believe that SOI® will not just accelerate the efforts of early adopters but, more importantly, will empower and activate previously reluctant or purely commercial organizations to start a journey they now know they must take if they are to thrive in the longterm. It will be hard work but I really hope that with this book Neil will succeed in his mission to accelerate progress. I particularly like the SOI® Learning Loops as a clever mechanism for checking the health and vitality of an organization's SOI® with all its constituents – measurement so often being the Achilles heel for change management programs.

All that remains is for me to wish you the best of luck. I truly believe that if you commit to becoming the company your colleagues, customers and community want you to be, this playbook can take you there.

Julian Richer

INTRODUCTION

Included in these pages is a complete toolkit that will help you change your business for good and deliver what an increasing number of employees, consumers and investors are demanding.

If you have picked up this book I'm guessing you're interested in making a difference. I'm guessing that you're thinking business as usual isn't going to change anything, and I'm guessing that you're looking for something that might just do this. Welcome to my world.

Seeking answers

As far back as I can remember I have been consumed by a conflict that exists in my heart and mind that pits the way things are against the way things could be. I was lucky enough to find a solution for my frustration in my early twenties through design. Soon after graduating with a degree in graphic design, I was bold enough to found and lead my own design consultancy and for the next ten years I happily scratched my itch. But it wasn't enough and what I gradually realised was that design alone wasn't changing things enough for me personally. While I'm proud to say I had some very satisfied clients and helped create a wonderful sense of shared achievement amongst my team, I wasn't satisfied myself.

Graphic design felt somehow too superficial and its impact too fleeting. I needed to do more.

The pursuit of this desire led me across the bridge that exists between graphic design and strategy and into the world of corporate branding. I sold my design business and joined the world's biggest and, financially, most successful branding consultancy of the time, WPP's Enterprise IG. For three years I worked around the world for big-name corporate clients in the banking, energy, pharmaceutical, infrastructure, mining and technology sectors. The life was fast-paced, demanding, sometimes glamorous, very well paid and ultimately important – at least it seemed so at the time. And then it all, quite suddenly, collapsed. The dot-com stock market bubble burst and, at the exact same time, my belief in anything that I was doing was right. The company I was working for was a fee-generating machine churning out generic brand promises, brand values and brand identities (logos) with little thought or under-standing of what kinds of internal cultures the bolting on of such empty vessels would create or the sharp practices it would mask. I only need to name some of the clients I worked for: Arthur Andersen, BP, Merrill Lynch.

It took some time to reset, but dropping out of the corporate system completely and moving to New Zealand allowed me the time to look with fresh eyes from a distance and consider the way things were and the way they could be. I carried on working in the private sector, but gradually my work for human rights organizations, international NGOs, various parts of the UN, billionaires foundations, and sustainability agencies consumed more and more of my time, thinking and reading.

Putting all my experiences together with a more complete world view and an ever-growing concern for where we are heading left me with all sorts of unanswered questions, but it was the initially cursory registration of three simple words that brought everything sharply into focus for me: Single Organizing Idea. I found these three words in a bestselling business book called *Good to Great* written by Jim Collins in 2001. Single Organizing Idea is not capitalised in Jim's book as it is here. It is not a tool, nor an approach,

just three words that make up a sentence, but for some reason, they stuck out to me and I realised at that very moment that here was a solution to many of the questions I had in my head.

My intrigue led me to see if Single Organizing Idea was a 'thing' and that, in turn, led me to the 20th-century philosopher Isaiah Berlin who had expanded on the concepts described by an ancient Greek poet named Archilochus who wrote a fable about "The Hedgehog and the Fox". Jim referenced the fable to explain his hedgehog business concept. 'Hedgehogs', he said, "simplify a complex world into a single organizing idea, a basic principle or concept that unifies and guides everything. While foxes never integrate their thinking — their opportunist tendencies means they pursue many things at the same time."

The need for radical change
The dot-com bubble changed my life and the direction of it. It was a time of great uncertainty and it caused many people to pause and revaluate what is important. But for most, a return to business as usual was what they knew and what they did just as most did following the Global Financial Crisis of 2008. As I

write this we are faced with another global crisis in the shape of a pandemic that many more people are saying will be a transformative event that changes how things are done. The outbreak of COVID-19 is, without doubt, the most serious event to have happened in my lifetime. But what concerns me most are the catastrophic predictions related to climate crisis, the continuing discrimination and entrenched poverty in the name of profit that are destroying us and our planet.

We have the opportunity to change, but talking about it is different from actually doing something about it. Without the tools we have no chance.

'Bolt-on' brand promises, fluffy purpose declarations and tick box style corporate social responsibility reports are not the tools we need. We need tools that will bring about root and branch system change. Single Organizing Idea (SOI®) can't directly change the capitalist system we have created (that is in the gift of states and governments), but it can change the operating systems of the enterprises that feed it. The threat to our existence is real; the threat to business as usual undeniable. While you will find a few enlightened leaders calling for change and spouting about purpose, founding 'do-good tribes' and attending elite forums, the truth is that most are shackled to enterprises so big, profit-hungry and complex that breaking free of the status quo would be akin to going on hunger strike.

This book then is for the businesses that can change. The small and medium-sized enterprises that exist in the very backbone of our communities. The ones that can't afford the mega fees of the big salaried consultancies, which have no skin in the game and only the case studies of big businesses to explain.

What change takes

Included in these pages is a complete toolkit that will help you change your business for good and deliver what an increasingly vocal number of employees, consumers and investors are demanding. It is packed with step-by-step explanations that will help you discover, define and embed a Single Organizing Idea (SOI®) that will ensure every business decision you make contributes to an equitable future where everyone thrives, not just those at the top.

But let's be clear, what's not included is a silver bullet!

There are no shortcuts to progress. Make no mistake, changing for good is a significant undertaking. It's a challenge that has to be walked towards and will demand not just your time and resources but courage, collaboration, belief, empathy, commitment and, ultimately, leadership.

For some managers changing for good is an exciting prospect that can't come soon enough. For others, it's an unnecessary step into the dark that upsets the status quo and fills them with fear and trepidation.

No matter how compelling your SOI® is or how obvious the potential commercial benefits for your business and your stakeholders, without clear, determined and bold leadership you will fall short.

Old-fashioned top-down command and control style management won't cut it. What is required is open-minded leaders who understand their role as proactive facilitators capable of drawing on their personal sense of purpose to convince,

inspire and encourage those around them toward a brighter future. Setting out on that journey in the first instance requires leadership. Barak Obama borrowed a quote from the celebrated poet and civil rights activist Maya Angelou which I, in turn, am humbly borrowing from him: "Change will not come if we wait for some other person or some other time. We are the ones we have been waiting for. We are the change that we seek."

Though radical change is required to rid the world of what is destroying it, SOI® is itself not radical; as you will see, it's a simple common sense call to action that I have spent the last 20 years collaborating with others to test and refine to ensure it remains just that – fluff and jargon-free, actionable common sense.

Just picking up this book you are demonstrating the kind of curiosity that is required to change the way things are to the way they could be. I wish you luck and hope that this book helps bring you success.

Neil Gaught
London, August 2020

CONTENTS

4.0

ALIGN

How to implement your SOI® These tools will help you align with your SOI® and start making a difference to your business performance and society.

5.0

MEASURE

How you measure the impact of your SOI® These tools will help you understand the difference your business is making in real time.

6.0

APPENDIX

Gain more from SOI® Learn about ongoing support, how to get involved and a special bonus.

SINGLE

ORGANIZING

IDEA

1.0

S O I ® 1 0 1

SOI® Explained In this section, you will find all you need to know about SOI®, what it is, how it can help and what's needed to get started.

1.1 BEYOND PURPOSE

Let's be clear from the start: having a purpose isn't going to save the world, nor is it going to save your business.

Twenty years ago, when I was working for WPP and the world's largest branding agency, I was in the right place at the right time to witness the birth of brand purpose. "A purpose that will unite over 100,000 people" was the grand declaration made to his staff by its CEO Lord John Browne when he reframed British Petroleum to stand for a purpose: "Beyond Petroleum".

Along with BP's new purpose was a new set of values. But just as the purpose was part of the emperor's new clothes, so were the values. Asked about BP's values after the first of three catastrophic events, which culminated in the largest oil spill into the sea ever recorded, one employee told *Fortune* magazine in 2006, "The values are real, but they haven't been aligned with our business practices in the field."

BP's purpose was a masquerade. At its core wasn't a call to action to go beyond petroleum

on behalf of people and the planet but instead the ceaseless and senseless pursuit of an insatiable desire to grow and grow. The human struggles that this addiction caused are dramatically captured in the movie blockbuster *Deepwater Horizon*.

BP is like many businesses today that claim to have a purpose that makes them good for the world. But the truth is they are more influenced by the idea of having a purpose than actually acting on one. In essence, growth remains the core strategy; control comes from the top-down, targets are still set in the short term and progress is measured and described in financial numbers.

To their credit, unlike the purpose agnostic squatters, some of these purpose-influenced businesses do go beyond compliance, with some proactively not only supporting good causes but also dreaming up ones of their own to make a contribution. But this kind of purpose is neither the reason for their existence nor their strategy.

Purpose has become a sort of life raft that many of the world's biggest businesses are clinging to.

As you will discover, a business with an SOI® at its core is a very different beast.

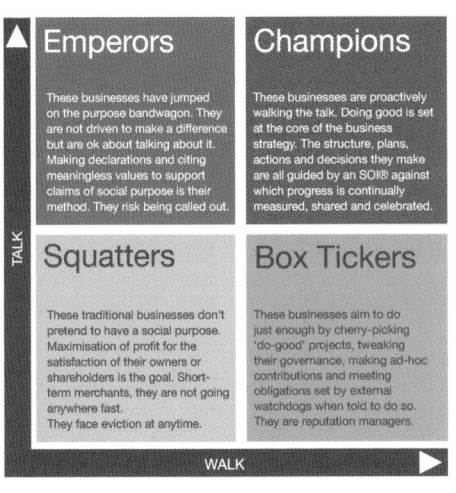

Walking the talk There is a big difference between what gets said and what gets done. Turning a blind eye, not totally committing or just doing enough is a risky business.

Purpose agnostic	Purpose influenced	SOI® aligned
Pyramidic, silo structure	Pyramidic, silo structure	Flat, networked ecosystem
Top-down control	Top-down control	Self-organizing operating system
Supply-chains	Supply-chains	Value-chains
Short-term profit focus	Short-term profit focus	Long-term thrive focus
Employee indifference	Employee engagement	Employee fulfilment
Efficiency and process driven	Brand comms and CSR combine to win preference through selected customer 'experiences'	Call to action at the core
Reputation management		Encourages and facilitates a regenerative, circular ecosystem
Sales and marketing communications aimed at winning customers	Brand promises and brand values drive 'surface' culture	Deep, holistic commitment to meaningful values
CSR 'bolted on'	'Win-win' projects make money	Collaboration culture
Success is financial	Sophisticated market share measuring tools	Sophisticated alignment/impact measuring tools
	Success is financial	Success is sustainable
Fit for little	Fit for some	Fit for all

Stuck in the middle with you. Many companies state that they have a purpose but the evidence suggests that not all of them act on it. Big businesses have been called out. Citi, Goldman Sachs and BlackRock have each been challenged by activists to deliver what they promised in a Business Round Table pledge to expedite stakeholder capitalism in August 2019.

1.2 THE POWER OF A SINGLE STRATEGY

SOI® has three qualities accurately described in its name. It does exactly what it says on the tin:

1. Single: **one**
2. Organizing: **systematically coordinated**
3. Idea: **concept that benefits all**

One single strategy
I first learned about strategy during my time in the military. My many experiences in business and my evolving view of the world have added some colour but not altered my thoughts about it: It means FOCUS.

Strategy is, in essence, a simple affair wrapped in a mystery and served up as an enigma by expensive, salaried consultants that make it unnecessarily complicated. Its perceived expense is one reason why so many SMEs don't have one!

But you don't have to buy one, as you will discover in this book, and having the right one is going to make a world of difference to your business and, intentionally, a difference to the world.

Strategy goes like this: To progress I need to get from point A to B. To put it another way, by getting from point A to B I will have achieved my objective. Strategy then is a plan of action that when communicated is a call to action. And that's it!

Of course, how you ensure you arrive at your objective depends on having the right strategy. And how you discover that is described in detail in the second part of this book – spoiler alert – and that bit isn't too hard either.

But that's for later. At this stage, the first point is to recognise that strategy is simple. In fact, the simpler the better. The second point, and this is important, is that if your business is to succeed in the future, it must concentrate and totally focus on one single strategy. That might sound crazy, but the fact is while some SMEs have no strategy whatsoever, many are trying in vain to achieve two often competing ones.

Fundamentally, the reason why many big businesses are not fit for the future is because they are either being led by the objective of

making money at all cost, or they are being tied in knots by trying to achieve that outcome whilst, at the same time, managing parts of the business which are intent on pursuing a separate strategy that leads to all sorts of embarrassing shenanigans.

SOI® ties both the economic and social strategies into one single strategy, the outcome of which is not only commercially sustainable, but also meaningful for those wishing to find fulfilment in what the business does. SOI® is about total commitment and being organized around a single plan of action the progress of which is measured. It's not about ticking a box or having a cheesy 'doing well by doing good' style purpose statement. SOI® is the means to get on and do it.

1.3 SELF-ORGANIZING SYSTEM

Systematic coordination

The way traditional businesses are organized limits their potential and ability to rise to the challenges set by climate change and the many other global challenges of our time that are captured in the UN's Sustainable Development Goals (SDGs).

To focus your business on helping achieve the goals that are going to make a difference to the world will require a major rethink of how your business is organized and operated.

The second element of an SOI® helps define how your business will work, how it is structured and the governance of that structure.

In hierarchical businesses, people and functions are organized around and directed by the wants and desires of the people at the top of the business and specifically the boss (CEO). With the average tenure of a CEO being five years and his (they are mainly men) wants and desires being invariably linked to short-term financial rewards, you can see why businesses with silos competing against each other to make the boss

happy are a major barrier to any kind of long-term, coordinated progress.

SOI® replaces the CEO as the organizing principle. It flattens the pyramid and redistributes power across the entire business and the ecosystem that it supports. In doing so, SOI® liberates people, enabling them to pursue a sustainable objective that comes from the beating heart of the business and not the temps at the top of it.

The best way to visualise the practical arrangements and efficiencies of an SOI®-led business versus a traditional one is to think about roundabouts versus traffic lights. Whereas as a roundabout system encourages and enables collaboration and coordination – basically freedom and shared responsibility – a remotely controlled traffic light system promotes an authoritative, dehumanising operation that dictates what starts and what stops.

I should add that just because the SOI® replaces the CEO as the organizing principle this doesn't

mean there isn't the need for leadership – there is, in spades! But the bottom line is that people organize themselves around an SOI®, not under a boss.

SUSTAINABLE DEVELOPMENT GOALS

Helping put the ball in the net The Sustainable Development Goals address the global challenges we face, including those related to poverty, inequality, climate change, environmental degradation, peace and justice. https://www.un.org/sustainabledevelopment/sustainable-development-goals/

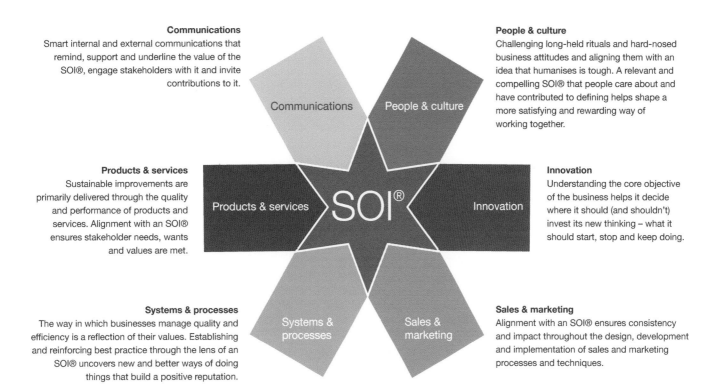

Communications
Smart internal and external communications that remind, support and underline the value of the SOI®, engage stakeholders with it and invite contributions to it.

People & culture
Challenging long-held rituals and hard-nosed business attitudes and aligning them with an idea that humanises is tough. A relevant and compelling SOI® that people care about and have contributed to defining helps shape a more satisfying and rewarding way of working together.

Products & services
Sustainable improvements are primarily delivered through the quality and performance of products and services. Alignment with an SOI® ensures stakeholder needs, wants and values are met.

Innovation
Understanding the core objective of the business helps it decide where it should (and shouldn't) invest its new thinking – what it should start, stop and keep doing.

Systems & processes
The way in which businesses manage quality and efficiency is a reflection of their values. Establishing and reinforcing best practice through the lens of an SOI® uncovers new and better ways of doing things that build a positive reputation.

Sales & marketing
Alignment with an SOI® ensures consistency and impact throughout the design, development and implementation of sales and marketing processes and techniques.

A holistic solution Instead of organizing around functions, SOI® reengineers your business so the functions organize around the SOI®, making it less siloed, top-down and more focused.

1.4 IDEAS FOR GOOD

A concept that benefits all
All businesses start off with an exciting idea.

The problem is that ideas are fragile, they need to be taken care of, fed and nurtured. All too often ideas are quickly lost as the initial objective and its benefits are overwhelmed by the day-to-day mechanics of running a business. Eventually, the dream first imagined becomes a distant memory, occasionally visited when the corporate calendar has time.

It doesn't have to be that way. The third feature of SOI® is the supremacy of your core idea.

SOI® puts your idea at the very heart of your business, and keeps it there by making its realisation your single-minded objective, ensuring everything your business does, every decision it makes and dilemma it seeks to resolve is guided by your core idea.

No matter the size of your business, with a sustainable idea at the core you have the opportunity to change the world and to change people's lives.

Great ideas excite people. The best ideas inspire; they compel people to think, to contribute and to share their own suggestions. The best ideas are meaningful and useful; they satisfy and they fulfil us. The best business ideas solve a problem.

The best ideas endure; they are resistant to marketing, technology and management changes. They endure because they matter and they matter because they are valuable.

I love this quote from Christopher Nolan, the storyteller and film director: "An idea can transform the world and rewrite all the rules."

Today we need many more ideas that are prepared to question the status quo and rewrite the rules. Ideas and businesses that can do more for less.

Identifying and defining an idea that can change the world is within your grasp and this book will help you do just that. It will also help you rewrite the rules of how you run your business to ensure that your idea stays front and centre of it.

© marketoonist.com. Reproduced with permission.

*Flat
There's no such thing as a totally flat organization. There has to be some form of command and control coming from somewhere and leadership is a key component of SOI®, as you will see. But high-performing, single-minded organizations can be very, very flat indeed. In such organizations everyone knows that they are contributing, there's a shared sense of ownership, and unnecessary top-down bureaucracy is avoided at all costs.

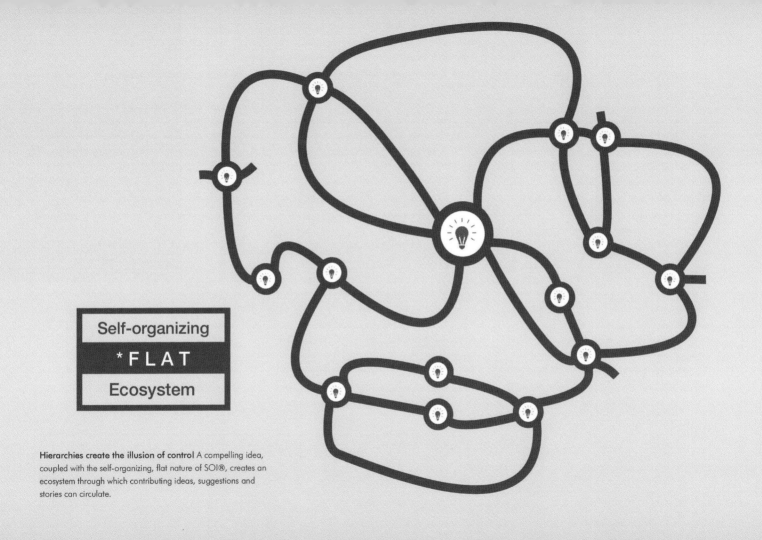

Self-organizing

*FLAT

Ecosystem

Hierarchies create the illusion of control A compelling idea, coupled with the self-organizing, flat nature of SOI®, creates an ecosystem through which contributing ideas, suggestions and stories can circulate.

1.5 EVERYONE BENEFITS

The graphic on the opposite page illustrates what alignment with a meaningful SOI® will improve, attract and deliver for your business.

SOI® unlocks the door to a host of positive outcomes, some of which will be experienced immediately and some later. Let's take a brief look at one example from each of the lists to illustrate what you can expect to experience inside and outside your business.

Firstly, internal improvement. Your staff will immediately experience and sense being part of a new and meaningful movement that matters not only to the wellbeing of the business but to their own personal wellbeing and the wellbeing of their families. It may sound a bit OTT, but I have sat with people who have literally cried with joy when the SOI® they have helped identify and define has been revealed and explained to them. This stuff can touch hearts in just the same way as the extraordinary joint efforts did that united people during COVID-19.

Next, externally. While some factors and functions aligned with your SOI® will take time to bring on stream, discussions with stakeholders about the value of your SOI® will prompt and motivate partners to contribute suggestions and even realign their activities to complement yours. An immediate side benefit of SOI® is that those who don't or cannot contribute positively are quickly exposed and you can let them go. A small business I worked with that realigned its business with a sustainable SOI® brokered brand new relationships within weeks, and also attracted new ideas, new people and saved costs. This stuff touches minds too and the logic applied leads to better ways and new efficiencies.

Over the longer term your SOI® and, in particular, the approach to innovation I describe later in this book, will help you and your partners uncover new products and services. Your SOI® will also stand a greater chance of attracting support from long-term investors with an eye on the future, who are turning their backs on traditional business and seeking to secure new sustainable opportunities for themselves or their clients.

Traditional businesses see success as growth – and some will pursue it at all costs. Growth is important to businesses aligned with an SOI® too, but the aim is to thrive commercially and develop sustainably, not to compete on financial terms and pursue growth for the sake of growth. This 'less is more' way of thinking about profit counters unnecessary consumerism, focuses minds, and delivers what is needed rather than what is desired.

The best and brightest amongst Greta Thunberg's generation are not interested in working for money, they want to do something that matters to them and the world. Your SOI® will attract them, benefit them and benefit their careers and their chances of making a difference.

Economic strategy

Social strategy

Improves

Procurement choices

Employee retention

Innovation

Reputation

Transparency

Organizational efficiency

Risk management

Sales and marketing

Supply-chain management

Stakeholder engagement

Attracts

The best employees

New ideas

New partnerships

Long-term investors

Lower cost of capital

Delivers

United ecosystem of stakeholders - value chain facilitation

Short and long-term value creation for both shareholders and society

Sustainable prosperity

Businesses determined to make a difference attract and unite people; they innovate and pioneer new efficiencies, enjoy long-term investment, and secure the support of their customers and the communities they aim to serve.

1.6 YOUR GUIDING STAR

SOI® acts as your guiding star. It's the reference point or touchstone against which every part of your business and the ecosystem it contributes to can measure progress and improve efficiencies and performance.

An SOI® will help you navigate through the process of changing your business for good, help solve ethical dilemmas, guide decisions, and settle governance policies. It will encourage people to think about opportunities, parameters and constraints, how they can work better together, and what they can expect from each other.

As understanding of your SOI® grows so will people's commitment to it. The approaches and tools set out in this book encourage involvement and provide opportunities for collaboration and celebration.

But let's be clear, this is not going to happen overnight and the path to progress is not a straight one. Everyone is different and it will take time for people to adjust and realise the power and potential of the SOI® to make a difference

to your business and to them personally. Some may never do so, and it may be the case that you need to let some of these self-serving people go.

The fact is, SOI® is not a silver bullet. Embedding an SOI® is challenging, questioning long-established conventions, taking on indifference, and convincing people of a better way takes leadership, patience and guts.

The good news is that as well as being a guiding star, your SOI® is also a call to action. The best SOIs are simple, direct, clear and determined. These attributes will give clarity and meaning to your leadership. Explanations about what your business is doing and why will always be anchored in truth and what actually matters with an SOI® at the core.

The other bit of good news is that even the most cynical people shift their opinion. In my experience, it is often the most vocal defenders of the status quo, the ones that seem the most resistant to change, who become the greatest champions of SOI® once it is implemented.

Measuring progress is important and you will see later that accountability is a key feature of an SOI®-aligned enterprise. Understanding where your business is going, how fast, and who and what is contributing to your efforts are important facts to know.

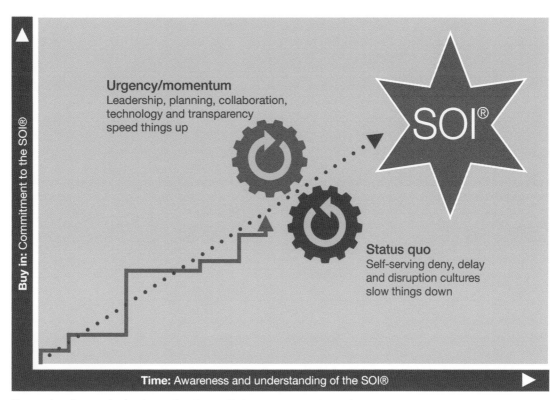

There are lots of stars in the sky Choosing the right one will help you navigate towards your objective.

1.7 SOI® AT WORK - EXAMPLES

Almost any business can change and be a force for good if the people who run it so desire. Admittedly, if you're busy manufacturing parts for weapons, or your survival is reliant on destroying the environment or exploiting people, you're amongst the exceptions and you will need to keep going with the PR purpose spin.

As you can see from the list opposite, it's not just businesses that can benefit from an SOI®. Indeed, SOI® thinking has been applied to international NGOs, not-for-profit associations, one-off projects and locations.

The size of a business doesn't matter either. New Zealand tech business DataTorque has less than thirty employees. That said, it has literally millions of stakeholders all over the world. In enabling small countries to successfully collect taxes rather than rely on foreign aid, what DataTorque does and how it does this boils down to an SOI® that helps guide what 'collective success' looks and feels like.

Catholic Relief Services is one of the world's largest international NGOs with thousands of employees working across the planet. Regardless of the country they work in, their individual role, or indeed their faith (the vast majority are Muslims and, indeed, some don't follow any faith at all) the one thing they share is their belief in a better world.

Dutch logistics company Europool System is the biggest distributor of fruit and vegetables in Europe with an annual turnover in excess of €1bn. Each and every day, its operations are governed and directed by a shared understanding of the value 'maximising circular solutions' for the benefit of all shareholders. The SOI® has driven the development of new products and services, helped attract new talent, and won the firm admiration and recognition as a pioneer in its field.

Fashion is a contentious sector and I have first-hand experience of how willing big businesses are to piggyback off the back of a fluffy purpose promise, some slick branding, and a bit of 'do-gooding'. That's not the case with Britain's Community Clothing nor Canada's Norden. Both have powerful SOI®s at the core of their businesses that are creating pride by making a real difference to people's lives and the world around them.

Not all big businesses are set in their ways and some have managed to adapt or are busy adapting. I suggest that you have a look at PepsiCo (Performance with Purpose), IBM (Smarter Planet) and Unilever's Sustainable Living Plan (USLP). As the driving force behind USLP, Unilever's recently retired CEO, Paul Polman, demonstrated many of the leadership characteristics that are required to drive real change and take on the status quo, and not just in his own business.

SINGLE ORGANIZING IDEA (SOI®)	TYPE	ENTERPRISE
Enabling Change	Inclusive business network/platform	IBAN
Partners for Good	American INGO	Global Communities
Collective Success	New Zealand tax collection technology	DataTorque
Promote and Protect	Global human rights organization	UNHCR - GANHRI
Pride	British clothing manufacturer	Community Clothing
Believing in Better	American faith-based INGO	Catholic Relief Services
Mining the Resource. Enriching the Nation*	Anglo/African mining company	Debswana
Cultivating Wholesome Food	French food products company	Danone - Blédina
Building Better Communities	New Zealand construction company	Hawkins
Assuring Confidence	American accreditation organization	ABET
Waste	Canadian apparel manufacturer	Norden
Maximising Circular Value	Dutch logistic company	Euro Pool System

This list of twelve is a representative sample. I have worked with many other companies around the world but due to confidentiality restrictions cannot list them here. *I was working with WPP when this was coined in 2001. It wasn't defined as an SOI® but it was based on the truth and subconsciously changed me and my goals – two years later, I was developing SOI®.

1.8 A VERY HUMAN APPROACH

Whether you plan on building a business, going on holiday or buying a car, if you're smart you'll do the research, identify the best option, and then use BOTH your heart and your mind to take the right course.

The best SOI®s are born out of honesty, human collaboration, empathy, the pursuit of truth, and total transparency. In an age of 'fake everything' that is not only important, it's critical.

An SOI® is not made up on the back of an envelope, it's discovered and it's going to take time to carry out (actually how long depends on the size of your business). It's also going to take commitment and leadership. It may even mean facing up to uncomfortable truths, as well as achieving and measuring results in a way that you may not have done before. More than anything, it's going to take trust. Trust in the people around you and trust in people from outside your business. It is going to be their ideas and their collaboration that will lead you to your SOI® and, ultimately, it will be they who make it a reality.

Starting off

You should bring together a small SOI® team if you can. As the business owner or CEO, you will need to be heavily involved but you should nominate someone who can lead the team. In it, you should have someone with good project management and people skills. It's a great opportunity for a rising star with energy to hone their skills and experience. You may want someone from outside your business to take you through the process and keep your team on track. Be careful who you choose. Ideally, you need a mentor who can both inspire and hold you and your team to account. The best advisors are straight talkers with a broad range of experiences, knowledge, skills and intuition. The person you choose should be a future thinker but not an idealist; able to weigh what is possible against what is practical.

The first task of the team is completing the identifying phase of the process. This involves using the tools and approaches described in the next part of this book to carry out a thorough analysis of your business – where you are now and where it can go.

Like any project, success comes through proper planning and preparation and to aid your team with this, an SOI® workbook is available that includes a project Gannt chart template and a description of each task broken down into its:

- Objective
- Process
- Outcomes
- Timing

You might also want to name your project. One of the first tasks for your team is to find a name that is neutral but uplifting. Once you have the plan – and the name – you're ready to start the exciting process of discovering your SOI®, and changing your business for good.

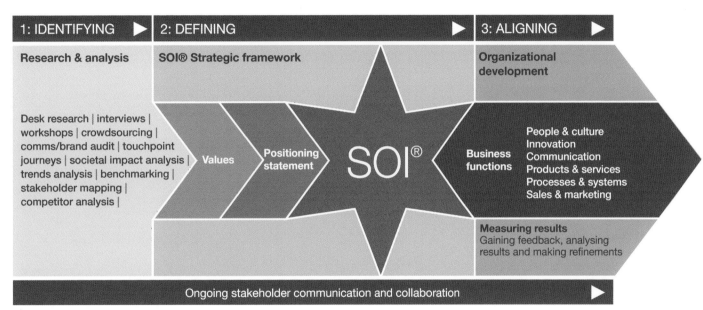

1: IDENTIFYING ▶ **2: DEFINING** ▶ **3: ALIGNING** ▶

Research & analysis

SOI® Strategic framework

Organizational development

Desk research | interviews | workshops | crowdsourcing | comms/brand audit | touchpoint journeys | societal impact analysis | trends analysis | benchmarking | stakeholder mapping | competitor analysis |

Values

Positioning statement

SOI®

Business functions

People & culture
Innovation
Communication
Products & services
Processes & systems
Sales & marketing

Measuring results
Gaining feedback, analysing results and making refinements

Ongoing stakeholder communication and collaboration ▶

A process that rewards as you progress Identifying, defining and ultimately aligning your business with an SOI® is a rewarding and meaningful experience that engages hearts and minds, throws up valuable insights, and builds your systems along the way.

KEY POINTS

✓ The threat to business-as-usual is undeniable. SOI® is a proven toolkit for those with the ambition and commitment to change.

✓ SOI® is needed because a fluffy purpose statement is not enough to bring financial and social strategies together in ways that ensure coherence and commercial success.

✓ SOI® replaces the top-down organization model with a decentralised self-organizing model that inspires people to contribute to a business that benefits everyone while achieving commercial success.

✓ SOI® guided businesses stand out; they attract and retain the most ambitious talent, uniquely attract long-term investors and benefit from naturally cultivated, deeply loyal customers.

✓ In an ever more vigilant world, purpose washing and compliance box-ticking is not going to cut it. Sustainable progress and its benefits will only go to those who earn it through application and grit.

YOUR NOTES

SINGLE

ORGANIZING

IDEA

2.0

IDENTIFY

How to identify your SOI® Your SOI® already exists. In this section you will find the tools and methods you need to discover it.

2.1 DESK RESEARCH

In shaping an SOI® that will ensure your business is fit for the future you firstly need to orientate where you are today and then identify future events and mega trends that are likely to affect where you want to go in the future.

I best describe this as looking at the climate. If a weather forecast describes the impact of short-term variation in atmosphere in days and weeks, then climate predictions describe what factors and events might affect the weather over the next thirty years.

Some events will be very specific to your business sector. What new product and service developments are likely to be launched? What will be the value of these new products and services, how will they differ from what is on offer today, and why will people consume them are other key questions you will want to consider.

In tandem, what new rules and policies are likely to be imposed, and how will regulation effect trading conditions, the expectations of future employees, and preferences of consumers and investors?

Two overriding factors that will change all businesses are technology and sustainability. What will be the impact of either on your business?

Directing your team to look at these factors will give you a view of the future; its opportunities as well as challenges. Most importantly, it will give you a social and economic reading against which to later judge and test your SOI® options.

Benchmarking
An experienced external advisor will bring knowledge from other sectors. Identifying and comparing best practice from other areas helps establish not only what is possible, but also how it might be achieved.

Benchmarking is a great way to mitigate risk. Investing time and effort in gathering success stories from other industry sectors not only provides reassurance but also helps explain the advantages and challenges of change. Adopting or adapting what has been successful elsewhere can give comfort to those people in your business who are either averse to or nervous of change. Of course, the benchmarking examples have to be relevant, but when you consider the objective of identifying and defining an SOI®, you may be surprised how diverse those examples might be. For example, a mixture of first-hand knowledge and researched successes and failures gathered from the private sector like GE, Vodafone, IBM, Starbucks and Unilever helped me stretch the thinking at one of the largest international NGOs on the planet to understand what was possible.

The results of the research can be written up into a report, but the best option is to boil everything down into a slide deck that concludes with a round-up of the findings and – most importantly – key insights.

SOI® PESTLE analysis

Factors	Key question	Step 1: List trends	Step 2: List implications for your business	Step 3: List key insights to help create an overall premise
POLITICAL	How may government and other political factors impact my business?			
ECONOMIC	What economic trends could have an impact on my business?			
SOCIAL	What are the emerging social and demographic trends?			
TECHNOLOGICAL	What technological innovations could affect the market?			
LEGAL	What changes in legislation could impact my business?			
ENVIRONMENTAL	What ecological aspects influence the business?			

Doing your homework will save you time and costs Desk research basically involves collecting data from internal and external sources.

2.2 WORKSHOPS

Workshops are a critical ingredient of an SOI® project. They help uncover what is in the hearts and minds of your staff and key stakeholders.

The outcome of the workshops are insights that will help identify future aspirations, as well as the current strengths and weaknesses of your business through others' eyes.

For over 20 years, I've successfully engaged and gleaned the thoughts and feelings of people through the workshop format described here. Regardless of their roles, the industry they work in or the country they live in (I've run workshops in 40+countries), I've found that the most fruitful approach is an open one that encourages human interaction and self-discovery.

Setting a context based on what is happening in the world and then running exercises that allow staff to express their concerns and aspirations as individuals, in teams and, finally, as an entire group can be extremely rewarding.

Without exception, every workshop I have ever run has identified a gap between how staff perceive their business today and how they would ideally like to perceive it in the future. Sometimes that gap is small and sometimes it is large, but in every single case there is a gap and a desire for 'better'.

The transparent and collaborative nature of SOI® workshops creates goodwill and builds 'buy-in' into the project.

The number of workshops and the time taken to complete this part of the process depends on the size and geography of your business. The maximum number of people in a workshop is 20. A timetabled program needs to be worked out. You might run simultaneous workshops over a single 72-hour period or alternatively hold them over a period lasting some weeks. It really depends on your resources and the nature of your business.

Overview
Each workshop takes half a day and comprises of a presentation followed by three exercises. Approximately three weeks before the workshop participants are sent an invitation. The invitation sets out the reason for the SOI® project, the timing and location of the workshop, along with preparation instructions for the first exercise.

Presentation *10 minutes*
The presentation should have the energy of a TED keynote: informative, educative and enjoyable. Importantly, it's not about persuasion, it's about setting the scene, grounding the participants and engaging their hearts and minds. It emphasises the importance of contributions and collaboration.

• Introductions.
• Changing world – what is changing and why; I use a clip from the BBC's *Blue Planet* here to get things going and explain the impact on society, business and the role of the UN's Sustainable Development Goals (SDGs).
• The power and potential of an SOI®.
• The project process.
• A short Q & A to confirm understanding.

Outputs
• Participants understand what is driving changes in the world of work.

• Participants understand the value of a strategy aligned with a Single Organizing Idea (SOI®) and the importance the project is being given by you.

Exercise 1 *Time depends on the group size*
Prior to the workshop each participant will have been instructed to bring along two objects (or pictures of them). The first object helps them to describe what they feel about the business today, and the second to describe what they think the business should be about in the future.

Each participant is given two minutes to present their objects to the group. The workshop facilitator records the descriptions on the whiteboard under the titles 'today' and 'tomorrow'. Within reason, debate during this exercise is not encouraged; the focus is on the opportunity for each individual to input their ideas in their own words without being challenged.

Outputs
• Insights into how individual participants actually and ideally view the business in their own words.

• Opportunity for participants to see how others view the business today and how they would like to see it in the future.
• Insight into the gap between actual (today) and ideal (tomorrow).
• Insight into the diversity of opinion. To what degree does a shared sense of purpose already exist in the business?

Photographs of participants describing their objects are useful in later communications promoting the progress of the SOI® project and, in particular, underlining the benefit of collaboration.

Exercise 2 *1.5 Hours*
The group is divided into equal teams. Each team nominates a leader and is given a deck of cards and a worksheet. The deck includes sets of images of animals, shapes, modes of transport and abstract items.

The teams are set two tasks to complete in break-out spaces:
1. Firstly, the teams are asked to identify from each set of cards an image they feel best

helps them to describe the qualities of their business today. For example, out of the animals set, a team may choose a horse as being the best representation of the business as it is admired, trustworthy, agile, competitive, noble, prestigious etc. The qualities are recorded by the team leader on the worksheet under the 'actual qualities' heading.

2. The exact same process is repeated a second time, but during this round the teams are asked to identify the 'ideal qualities' they collectively agree the business will need to ensure it is fit for the future.

On completion of the two tasks, the group is brought back together to share their choices and the reasons behind them. The actual and ideal qualities are recorded by the workshop facilitator on a whiteboard or flip chart as they are presented and the attributes are discussed. Data from all the workshops run during the project are recorded on a spreadsheet so that outcomes can be compared and similarities identified.

2.2 WORKSHOPS (cont.)

Outputs
- Insight into how teams actually and ideally see the business today.
- Indication of the latent qualities of the business today and the aspirational qualities of the business in the future.
- Indication of the gap between ideal and actual positioning and the degree to which a shared purpose exists (or doesn't).

Exercise 3 *60 minutes*
The group is divided into their teams again.

Worksheets listing 20 physical, tangible attributes (hard qualities) and 20 intangible attributes (soft qualities) are given to each team. In their break-out spaces the teams are asked to identify four qualities from the hard list and four qualities from the soft list that they think or feel the business needs to ensure it is fit for the future. The lists are compiled from the attributes identified during desk research, benchmarking and project-related interviews. Four blank spaces on each worksheet are provided should the teams wish to suggest an additional quality that is not listed.

Once the task is completed the teams are brought back together and a list of all the hard and soft qualities is written up on a flip chart. Led by the workshop facilitator, each of the qualities is discussed in turn. Specifically, the group is asked to consider to what degree they feel the business displays or is aligned with each of the qualities today. For example, 'empathy' may have been identified by the group as being an important quality to have in the future – but is it a quality the business already has?

Each quality is discussed and then ranked thus:

Positive (+): The business displays this quality.
Neutral (=): The business displays it somewhat.
Negative (-): This is not a quality of the business.

Outputs
- Insight into how the group actually and ideally perceives the business.
- Identification of key qualities.
- Insight into how the business is positioned currently.
- Indication on variance of opinion.
- Indication of depth of knowledge of the group.

SOI® Prompt card · SOI

CREATURE DECK

SOI® Prompt card · SOI

ABSTRACT DECK

SOI® Prompt card · SOI

TRANSPORT DECK

SOI® Prompt card · SOI

SHAPE DECK

Hands-on tools for the entire workshop are available.

2.3 INTERVIEWS

Interviews are gold dust. Held in confidence, interviews are the single most important element in the SOI® research phase. They are the very best method for looking under the bonnet and understanding what your business is truly about.

I have relied on them extensively in every engagement I've ever taken on and look forward to them eagerly. Interviews are the opportunity to look someone in the eye and uncover the truth about the business and their hopes and fears for it. With the right approach an interview will become a human interaction that reveals the values, qualities and motivations that drive the business. They will also provide an insight into the personal values and motivations of key individuals who have a stake in the business.

Notice that I talk about doing these interviews myself. This part of the project cannot be delegated to your internal team. To get real insight, interviewees need to feel free to express their thoughts and ideas to someone independent and skilled in asking the right people the right questions.

Identifying a broad spectrum of internal and external interviewees who represent opinion formers, as well as decision makers, is important. Interviews should be prioritised in a logical order so that the accumulated knowledge can be taken from one interview to the next. The CEO is naturally seen as the first port of call, but in many cases, I have found it useful to talk to other people in the organization first and then go to the CEO armed with some knowledge.

Interviews are not surveys and need to be taken up on an individual basis, with questions being developed and refined as the identifying phase progresses and knowledge is gathered and understood. Not all the questions listed opposite need to be asked. Indeed, only three or four questions may be asked during the hour that I recommend interviews should take. As well as gathering facts, stories, thoughts and feelings, interviews present an ideal opportunity to test support for ideas and potential challenges or resistance to them.

Just like the workshops, invitations to take part in interviews and thank you notes sent afterwards should be seen as opportunities to build interest in the SOI® project, build momentum and generate a sense of collaboration.

Interview questions

1. Background

1.1 What has made the business successful to date?

1.2 What is the reputation of the business – would you say it is positive, negative, or neutral? Does it vary for different stakeholders?

1.3 How is the reputation of the business managed? How do you think it should be managed?

1.4 What role do values play (amongst employees, leadership, stakeholders)?

1.5 How would you describe the leadership style of the business; how do things get done?

1.5 Are successes celebrated; what ones, when and how?

1.6 Is there pride in the business; what is the basis for it?

2. Sector

2.1 What is the reputation of the sector?

2.2 What is the future for the sector; to what

degree will the sector change; how will the sector develop?

2.3 Who/what is influencing that change?

2.4 Who are the opinion formers/leaders within the sector?

2.5 What factors do companies in the sector compete on?

3. Positioning

3.1 How is the business currently positioned? Has that always been the case? How should it be positioned in the future – the same/ differently?

3.2 Who do you regard as your most immediate competitors? How are the top three positioned; what are their strengths/ weaknesses?

3.4 Does the business ever collaborate with its competitors; how?

3.5 What are the preferences and expectations of your customers (stakeholders)?

3.6 How are the preferences/ideals or your customers (stakeholders), changing and developing?

3.7 How do you rank your stakeholders; who are the most important? which have the greatest influence on your business?

4. Future

4.1 What is the ambition of the business?

4.2 How will the business measure success in the future?

4.3 What are the critical factors that will affect the business' performance in the future?

4.4 What organizations do you most admire in the sector?

4.5 What organizations do you most admire outside the sector and why?

5. And finally…

5.1 Is there anything that I haven't asked you that you feel is important for me to know?

2.4 UNDERSTANDING STAKEHOLDERS

An article published by *The Financial Times* in 2004 defined a stakeholder as "anyone who can bugger up your business". The world has changed dramatically since then and I'd suggest you view stakeholders more positively as 'anyone who can help your business be a force for good'.

Understanding stakeholders' perceptions and their attitudes towards your business is vital to identifying a meaningful SOI®. Without understanding what concerns them – what they need, want and care about – your business cannot define and organize itself around an idea that matters and has value to them.

Stakeholders sit both inside and outside your business. They are part of the ecosystem that your business is part of. There are two types of you need to take a look at:

• **Primary stakeholders** have a stake in your business and its success directly affects them. Shareholders, employees, customers, consumers, owners, creditors, investors, governments (the tax collecting function), suppliers, partners, contractors and local communities all fall into this category.

• **Secondary stakeholders** have an indirect connection to your business and are largely external. But the actions and behaviours of your business can affect them and vice versa. They include unions, government (the regulation/policy-making function), trade associations, NGOs, advocacy groups, potential customers, potential employees, competitors, experts and analysts, education institutes, media, alumni, think tanks, researchers and the general public.

You may be surprised by the number and variety of stakeholders your business has. Though it cannot voice an opinion, the planet is a substantial stakeholder and, as it has shown increasingly, it can certainly bugger up businesses!

Stakeholders form their opinion of your business either through direct experience of your services or products, media messages you control, for example, marketing communications, and

messages you don't, for example, hearsay. Hearsay shared through social media channels is particularly potent and can have an immediate influence on the opinion of thousands of stakeholders. Stakeholders armed with smartphones and emojis to instantly rank and register their likes and dislikes are superseding qualified insights and real investigation. The bottom line is that what stakeholders think and feel about your business may not even be based on the truth, and their opinion may be changed in an instant.

Gathering a diverse group of stakeholders together to discuss their concerns, the perception they have of your business and the degree of influence they have will help identify issues, shape your SOI®, generate goodwill/support, and prioritise future actions. The matrix opposite shows the output from a simple exercise that asks three questions:

1. Who are our stakeholders?
2. How do they perceive our business as a force for good?
3. What are their concerns?

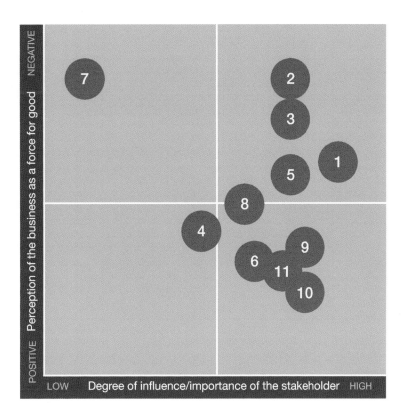

Identified stakeholder groups
1. Customers
2. Staff
3. Shareholders
4. Suppliers
5. Competitors
6. Media
7. NGOs
8. Associations
9. Sector think tanks
10. Policy makers/regulators
11. Government watchdogs

The first part of the exercise is to brainstorm all the stakeholders you can think of. This example shows a very short list of top-line stakeholder groups. Each of these groups can be broken down into types and then individual organizations. For instance, there are lots of types of media. You could easily identify 30+ stakeholders in a brainstorming session with colleagues.

Understanding who is in the ecosystem of which your business is a part will influence how, when, where and who you engage with in the future to help build a business for good. Note your competitors are amongst your stakeholders and possible future allies!

2.5 POSITIONING SPECTRUM

When marketing pioneer Walter Landor stated in the 1960s that "Products are made in the factory, but brands are created in the mind" he described in one sentence the potency of 'positioning'. Understanding the position that your business and others occupy in the minds of your key stakeholders is an important step toward creating a credible and successful SOI®.

Where traditional businesses will use positioning to gain competitive advantage, maximise sales and the consumption of their products or services, remember the purpose behind the work you are doing is to help your business, and the stakeholders that support it, thrive and prosper.

This means that while the approach to understanding how your business is positioned is similar, the goal of the exercise is completely different. The point of an SOI® is to gather people and resources around an idea that will make a difference to the world. Identifying who is already positioned to do this amongst two of your primary stakeholder groups (competitors and suppliers), and how they are reinforcing that positioning through communications and

actions, is a valuable exercise that will throw up insights, ideas, and even potential opportunities to partner further down the line.

Mapping

The positioning spectrum, illustrated on the opposite page, is a tool that will help you visualise where your key stakeholders sit relative to your business. To populate it, you need to:

1. Decide which key external stakeholders you want to review.
2. Identify and analyse their communications.

The analysis itself is a two-step process that starts by digging into your stakeholders websites:

Step 1
Proposition
The best place to look for this is under 'about us' on the organizations website menu. It may be immediately clear or you may need to look at a combination of mission, vision and purpose statements to decipher what is trying to be communicated, and whether it's consistent.

Marketing strapline
If they have one it will likely be tied up with the logo. Clever straplines sum up the purpose of the organization in a few catchy words.

Key messages
Key messages are cited reasons to believe in the business and its offers. To ensure they are remembered, smart organizations will repeat these messages often, consistently and in a variety of ways throughout their websites and other communication channels.

Qualities
Tangible qualities (a physical object such as a product) and intangible qualities (the experience gained by using that product), require some skill to identify, but you will notice the repetition of these attributes in sales propositions, value promises or organizational commitments and a list will emerge. Businesses that are focused and have clarity about who they are, and the value they deliver, will cite a few qualities. Those that don't will use a very long list indeed in the hope of covering all bases – or, more likely, simply because they don't know!

Step 2

This analysis compares and contrasts the look and feel and the tone of voice of the organizations you are reviewing; in a nutshell, their communicated personality. Again it takes some skill, but you can score your evaluation and rank their efforts against a best practice criteria that lists such things as: appeal, difference, memorability, engaging/interaction, simplicity, effectiveness, consistency across applications, cost efficiency, flexibility/ adaptability across media channels. Set a score against each criteria element like this:

- Negative score 1-3
- Neutral score 4-7
- Positive score 8-10

All of this information will not only help you map where these organizations sit relative to your own – you should carry out the exact same analysis of your own business – but also throw up insights into understanding what's effective, what's not, including opportunities to collaborate and support the ecosystem that you support and supports you.

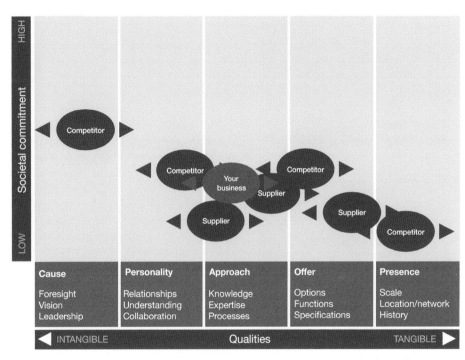

Positioned for success Organizations on the right of the spectrum quote tangible qualities, such as how big they are, how many things they sell, and what the things they sell do in their communications. Organizations on the left quote intangible qualities that explain why they do what they do. Many organizations today claim to be making some sort of contribution to society. The likely impact of that contribution can also be mapped on this spectrum once you have carried out the social contribution analysis explained in the next chapter.

2.6 SOCIAL CONTRIBUTION ANALYSIS

Carrying out a review of how you already contribute to society is a simple exercise that will throw up some interesting insights and aid you in identifying your SOI®.

In 2015 the publishing company Pearson identified 19 social issues that concerned stakeholders most through using a process that is not dissimilar to what I'm recommending here. The analysis they carried out contributed to 'The World's Learning Company', as it calls itself, by going beyond traditional Corporate Social Responsibility (CSR) to put 'helping people make progress in their lives through access to better learning' at the core of its business.

Assessing and mapping the nature of your current philanthropic and CSR* activities is a way to understand stakeholder concerns. Such analysis will bring clarity to the existing investment being made in society and the nature of it. Understanding the different objectives and types of contribution will help identify the strengths and weaknesses of your overall effort and gauge the impact of philanthropic giving versus CSR and rank 'no harm' policies against

'win-win' outcomes, such as those advocated by Michael Porter and Mark Kramer's Shared Value Initiative.

Step 1
Direct your appointed team to identify all the initiatives you are already investing in. Gathering documents will be the first step, but interviews with key individuals inside and outside your business may be required to get the full picture.

Step 2
Once they are collated use the Social Contribution Working Sheet to detail the social and business impact and costs associated with each contribution type.

Step 3
Finally, use the Social Contribution Summary Sheet to capture and rank the effectiveness of all your efforts in one place.

This information will not only help you identify what your SOI® could be but also help you to later focus and refine what you are already doing that fits with it – and what doesn't.

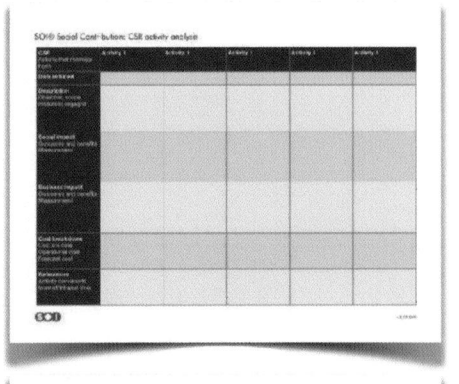

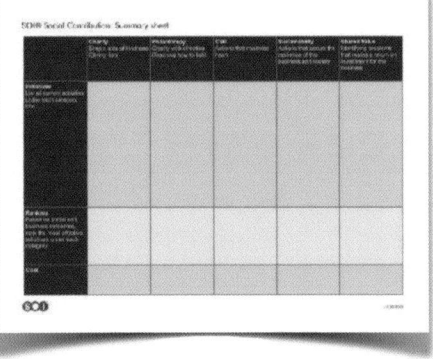

*ESG (environmental, social and governance) is a new term used by investors to evaluate CSR behaviour and determine the future financial performance of companies.

Charity	Philanthropy	Corporate Social Responsibility	Shared Value	Sustainability
Simple acts of kindness (Giving fish)	Charity with direction (Teaching how to fish)	Actions that minimise harm (Not overfishing)	Identifying societal problems that realise a return on investment for the business	Actions that assure the resilience of the business and society
Short-term Emotional intervention Focused on providing relief	Mid/long-term Focused on problem solving Cause-driven	Compliance with standards largely set by external agencies Responsible citizenship Triple bottom line reporting Building trust Protecting brand reputation 'Bolt-on' initiatives	Focus on profitability Transactional relationships pursued by some functions of the business Achieving competitive advantage Lowering costs Driving efficiencies and addressing deficiencies	Optimizing total alignment across all functions of the business to achieve a common ideal Building effective ecosystem relationships Innovation that meets the needs of all stakeholders Reducing risk for all **Core SOI® strategy**

Levelling up Having an SOI® at the core of your business sits squarely in the sustainability category. This is the highest level of commitment to society. In this category ALL your business functions and operating system are committed to delivering sustainable outcomes for your business, people and the planet.

2.7 TOUCH-POINT ANALYSIS

Heard the phrase 'first impressions count'? 'Touch-points' are the moments of truth when the rubber hits the road and your stakeholders experience what your business stands for.

At these critical moments, stakeholders almost instantly form an impression of your business that can last forever. Depending on how they think and feel about your business at that moment they may even take action! For instance, if the moment is a positive experience that appeals to their needs, wants or values, it is likely that they will want to repeat it and may even encourage others to do so too.

On the other hand, if the experience is negative and promises don't match realities, the opposite is true. They won't want to repeat the experience and may even warn others off.

An analysis of your stakeholder's experiences at these touch-points will not only help you pinpoint where your business engages with stakeholders but later help ensure the impact you seek to have is organized and consistent with your SOI® and the values that underpin it.

Touch-points are often linked to each other and can be looked at from the point of view of the different stakeholders you have identified. For instance, touch-points for employees include their experiences as a job candidate, the environment they work in, the tools they are asked to use, meeting formats, internal communications, company rituals and policies.

The analysis
As with many of the SOI® tools, the key to completing this exercise successfully is engagement and collaboration. Armed with SOI® Touch-point worksheets, teams representing different functions of your business can be briefed and facilitated to identify all the touch-points in their area, describe their impact, validate with stakeholders and prioritise their importance.

The opportunity to neutralise negative impacts and turn neutral experiences into positives ones is work for after you have defined your SOI®, but having done this exercise already you will be ahead of the game. You will have engaged some of your staff in the project, built more

goodwill, identified impact opportunities, involved key stakeholders in validating the thinking, and even have generated a list of where future priorities lay.

It may feel like a lot of work and, certainly, it will take time to do it well, but the benefits are plentiful. Not only will this analysis uncover social impact opportunities but it will also spotlight where greater efficiencies can be made and costs cut.

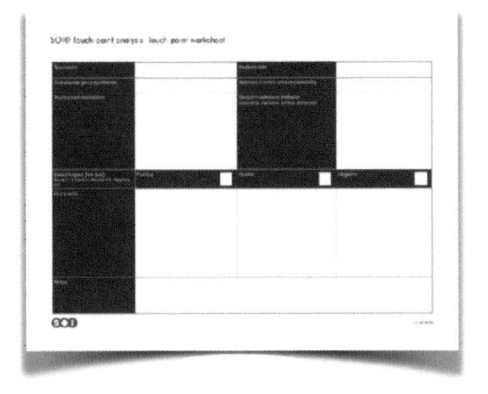

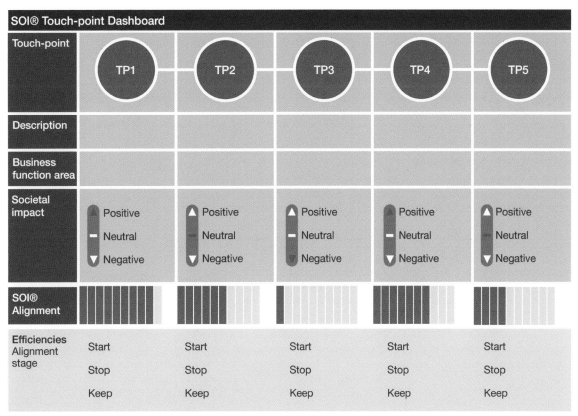

Listen up Setting up listening posts and regularly engaging your stakeholders with smart feedback mechanisms that monitor activity at these touch-points will help you to create a 'dashboard' of indicators that can be used to track progress, assess the health of your business and the degree of alignment with your SOI®.

2.8 CROWDSOURCING

Making people feel like they are part of what is happening and getting their input is an important key to success, but you can't interview everyone and there are only so many workshops you can run.

Surveys can include everyone but are both limited and limiting. Online crowdsourcing platforms, on the other hand, are a fantastic way to ensure no-one is left out in your quest to find the right SOI®. And the 'collective wisdom' of your stakeholders is a massive knowledge base that will bring ideas, clarity and unity. What people know and believe about shared business and social realities can be powerfully brought together through crowdsourcing.

Crowdsourcing companies like Synthetron, who I sometimes partner with to power my branded SOI® LikeMIND™ sessions, cleverly bring large groups of dispersed people together. Connected remotely, using their internet devices, it doesn't matter where in the world they are – only time zones do! A particular benefit is the anonymity that online crowdsourcing technology brings. It not only encourages straight talking but tackles the challenges that come with hierarchal business structures, giving everyone a safe space to speak their mind and a voice regardless of their status or role. We are all individuals with our own point of view, yet there are moments when our thinking is aligned and so, for a successful SOI®, it is not important who said what, but what was said and what was agreed.

A skilled moderator armed with the right questions can engage up to a thousand people in a one-hour session. In that time, not only will a large number of insights, ideas and suggestions have been harvested but the collective wisdom of the group will have ranked them, in effect, pushing the concepts they most like or agree with to the top of the list.

The process
- Identify the crowdsourcing platform you want to use. There are lots of choices online, including Synthetron. Check that you will end up with conclusions rather than just a vast amount of data you cannot possibly process objectively.

- Set the time and date of the session(s). Every business is different and every SOI® project is slightly different too. So decide if you want to have mixed participation drawn from across your ecosystem or if it will be more revealing to target specific stakeholder groups.

- Discuss and agree on the key questions to be asked by the session facilitator. Think about where there are gaps in your understanding and tailor the questions accordingly. Questions from the interview guide will help (see pages 29 and 30). Be sure to start with a question that everyone can answer to settle the group dynamic. And be careful not to overload the session.

Let the participants speak freely and you will find you quickly get to the heart of the matter.

- Invite participants. This is an opportunity to not only give them the log-on details but underline the benefits of your SOI® project. You will find that even those who cannot participate will be more engaged because they have been invited.

- Run the session with an open heart and open mind.

- Collate and present insights to your SOI® team.

- Thank the participants and acknowledge the value of their contribution. Great ideas are born out of collaboration. The more you can include them, for example, by sharing results and defining the next steps together, the more they will be onboard with your emerging SOI®.

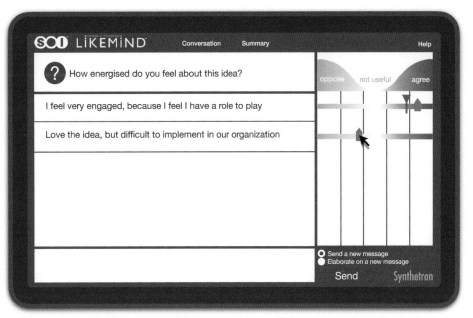

All together now It's possible to engage up to 1,000 people at one time in a Synthetron-powered LikeMIND™ session, but just a single one-hour session involving as few as 30 people will yield rich insights that will help you identify your SOI® and even how to bring it to life. Research the best system for you and your budget. COVID-19 has popularised online platforms that engage people and spawned lots of new ways to bring people and their ideas together.

2.9 BRINGING IT ALL TOGETHER

Facts and insights are the essential ingredients that are mixed together with intuition to create a successful SOI®. Having completed all the exercises you will have a lot of ingredients. The trick is to bring all this information together into one place so it can be properly reviewed, analysed and reasoned. This is best achieved through the creation of a slide presentation; a hypothesis that logically sets out the evidence and prepares the foundation for the defining of your SOI®.

The goal is to deliver the evidence in a compelling way that will explain what the facts point to, sets out what options exist, and recommends what route to take.

The presentation is a culmination of several months work, so not only does a decent amount of time need to be set aside for its delivery, the right people need to be in the room to hear it.

If you appointed a consultant to do the work then it will down to him or her to present the work they have done, the insights they have found and the recommendations they make. If

you created a team that shared the identifying tasks, then having them all play a role in presenting what they found makes sense.

Whoever presents, it is not something that can be rushed through. Logically setting out evidence backed up with hard facts that lay bare the truth of your business is a watershed moment and an opportunity to gain a deep understanding of the challenges, as well as the opportunities your SOI® will bring. You will be surprised by how much you didn't know about your business!

Identifying valuable sources of information, carrying out interviews and gathering research is the easy part. Analysing, understanding and drawing out insights from what's been gathered is somewhat harder. But the really hard part will be assembling it in a way that makes sense and leads to informed discussion and sound decisions.

There are limits to how much research can be done and there are also limits to what can be shared. Balance is absolutely critical in achieving recommendations that have both the authority

and the impact necessary to convince the audience that what is being presented is reliable and sufficient.

The hypothesis presentation is not only an opportunity to share insights, conclusions and recommendations, it is also an opportunity to generate more buy-in and build belief.

A lacklustre presentation that is delivered without conviction will not carry the day. The defining of your SOI®, the values that underpin it and the statement that will frame and position it for the future is an important moment.

The leadership team needs to be inspired to turn what they're being presented with into a reality. The aim is to arm them so that they can do that.

Presentations need to seize the moment, set the tone for the implementation and build momentum.

SOI®
PRESENTATION

Title slide
Project code name
Date

Objectives
Why

Contents
Section 1
Section 2
Section 3

SOI®
Methodology

Section 1
IDENTIFYING
Research and
analysis

Section
Introduction
Explanation
Scope
Objectives

Desk Research
Approach
Scope
Insights

Stakeholder
Analysis
Approach
Scope
Insights

Social Contribution
Analysis
Approach
Scope
Insights

Workshops
Approach
Scope
Insights

Touch-Point
Analysis
Approach
Scope
Insights

Crowdsourcing
Approach
Scope
Insights

Interviews
Approach
Scope
Insights

Research
Conclusion
Key insights

Positioning
Explanation
Scope
Objectives

Positioning
analysis
Stakeholders

Positioning
analysis
Your business today

Positioning options
Today v tomorrow

Positioning
recommendation
Fit for future position

Section 2
DEFINING
Values
Positioning statement
SOI®

Section
Introduction
Explanation
Objective

Positioning
statement
Solution

Value 1
Solution

Value 2
Solution

Value 3
Solution

Value 4
Solution

Single Organizing
Idea
Solution

SOI® Strategic
Framework
Solution

Summary
Conclusions
Benefits

Stress Testing
Instructions

Section 3
ALIGNING
Next steps

Section
Introduction
Explanation
Objective

Next steps
Explanation
Deliverables

Roadmap
Explanation

Presentation
summary
Key points

How it is and how it could be To ensure
everyone has the full picture fresh in their
minds it's best to present the research work
together with the defined SOI® solution. This
means one single presentation rather than two.

KEY POINTS

✓ Uncovering what is in the hearts and minds of your staff and key stakeholders will reveal the values, qualities and motivations that drive your business.

✓ Identifying the gap that exists between how your staff and stakeholders perceive your business today and how they would ideally like it to be in the future helps set the right intentions for your SOI®.

✓ Today, technology and sustainability are challenging every business in every sector. How will they impact yours? How do these and other factors provide opportunities for you to identify and tie together economic and social goals that will benefit your business and society?

✓ Positioning statements should no longer strive for a competitive advantage; indeed, they might reveal valuable opportunities to collaborate for the benefit of all.

✓ The 'Identify' phase involves methodical work and commitment, but when it's done well it inspires your leadership team, builds momentum and sets the tone for implementation.

YOUR NOTES

SINGLE

ORGANIZING

IDEA

3.0

DEFINE

How to create your SOI® Truth, logic and focus are the essential ingredients to creating a practical strategy that will last the test of time.

3.1 THE SOI® STRATEGIC FRAMEWORK

I can safely say I've met very few leaders who can recite their mission or vision statements. On the other hand, I've met plenty of people who think that it's all corporate bunk. Hardly surprising then that most of the best-laid plans of mice, men, and armies of expensive management consultants are busy gathering dust on leaders' shelves while people concentrate on what's needed to hit next quarter's financial targets.

But, as the saying goes, 'fail to plan and you plan to fail'.

The SOI® Strategic Framework is your core strategy, visually outlined in three boxes that contain your:

- Positioning statement
- Values
- Single Organizing Idea

Viewed together these three elements succinctly explain the why, what and how of your business. The framework defines your single-minded focus and gives you absolute clarity about what you are working to achieve. It's your roadmap to building and measuring your business success.

Your strategy is not a secret and neither is your SOI® Strategic Framework. It's THE key organizational communication tool that ensures all your stakeholders understand what your business is doing, why it's important, and how they can participate.

Your SOI® Strategic Framework is a clear and constant reminder of what matters most that everyone inside and outside your business can access, contribute to, and abide by every single day and through everything they do.

Everything you have learnt from the identify stage is now going to be distilled and condensed into two or three sentences, a few values, and a single idea that fills those three boxes. Sounds impossible? It's not, as you will discover over the next few pages.

What matters is the words you put in those three boxes. They will make a massive difference to you, your business, and the community that surrounds it for years, perhaps even decades, to come.

Get this bit right and you will have turned your extensive research into the foundation upon which you can build and measure your business success.

PS Your mission and vision statements – if you have them – might have been helpful during the research phase but now you can put them back on the shelf!

SOI® Strategic Framework

POSITIONING STATEMENT	CORE VALUES	SINGLE ORGANIZING IDEA
Your elevator pitch	Your commitments	Your guiding star
The positioning statement frames and explains the value of your SOI® to your business and to society in two or three pithy sentences. It's your elevator pitch.	Identified through research, these values underpin your SOI®. Each value is a commitment against which actions and ideas can be assessed and monitored. They are carefully selected to help ensure holistic and consistent alignment of your enterprise with the SOI®.	An SOI® is a simple and memorable call to action that is measured. Relevant, compelling and sustainable, an SOI® succinctly captures the core purpose of your enterprise. It's your guiding star.

3.2 YOUR CORE VALUES

There are no hard and fast rules when it comes to which part of your SOI® Strategic Framework you tackle first and in actual fact, you will find that it is a process of drafting, refining, redrafting, refining and redrafting again, all three elements simultaneously, until it's 'just right' to be presented and, crucially, tested. How long that takes depends on the quality of the research and the skill of your team or the individual who you set to do the task. It can take a day, or a week. My average is two days!

Having said there are no rules, my recommendation is that you start with the values.

Look up 'values' on the internet and you will find an array of definitions of what they are. Whole books have been written on the topic of values.

But let's keep it simple. In order for your business to successfully achieve its SOI® you need to understand values not as aspirations, nice-to-have culture shapers, or beliefs, but as solid unquestionable commitments that will ensure the delivery of positive, tangible outcomes.

Simply put, your core values are the cornerstones upon which your SOI® rests.

You have gone to great lengths to seek the ideas and thoughts of your employees and other stakeholders. Workshop exercises and interview questions have been specifically designed to identify, highlight and even test ideas on values. Research will have unearthed the cited values of your competitors, opinion formers and other stakeholders. While all this input is rich and valuable, make no mistake that the final set of values you settle on needs to be determined not just by what the crowd thinks but, ultimately, by what commitments you, as the leader of your business, believe need to be made to meet the call to action that your SOI® demands.

Your core values are the constant reminders of how things get done. They are the deeply embedded mechanism against which progress is measured and the basis of stories recounted and shared inside and outside your business.

Whatever their role or status, the performance of the people in your business, what they do and how they do it, will be guided, evaluated and rewarded against your core values.

For all the above reasons, it is critical that time is properly dedicated to arriving at a description of each value that is clear, directive and meaningful. Be inspired by the research but be equally determined in your resolve to define a values set that will make sure your SOI® is delivered.

Considering and testing whether you have got them right is the subject of the stress testing criteria explained on page 55.

Positioning statement	Core values	Single Organizing Idea
Our success is borne out of belief, a history of partnering and an understanding of what matters, and what doesn't. By being bold enough to dare and willing to care we help make everyone feel like winners.	**Cooperative** Our heritage shows that we get the best results when we work in solidarity. By being inclusive we unite and support joint efforts that enhance our collective strength. **Accountable** Our success is determined by the standards we set, the outcomes we pursue and the responsibility we take. By being straightforward, fair and answerable we underline we are dependable. **Attentive** By being tenacious, by having the confidence to open our minds and empathise, we create unique opportunities that allow compassion and understanding to push forward progress. **Courageous** Achieving better takes audacity and commitment. By relentlessly looking for improvement we challenge the status quo and shape new solutions and efficiencies.	Feel-good

This Strategic Framework example is based on a solution created for a global sports-inspired fashion business with a hundred year-old history. Research showed, especially amongst the business's' key consumer groups, that feeling good about the purchasing decisions they made was no longer just based on looks. This same sentiment was detected amongst employees and suppliers who were also questioning whether the business's' CSR efforts were having any genuine impact. The opportunity was to turn 'feeling good' into a simple but highly effective call to action that could drive the entire business toward a successful, commercially sustainable future.

3.3 YOUR POSITIONING STATEMENT

Your positioning statement is a cut-down summary that explains why your SOI® is valuable to people, the planet and society.

It's not a sales pitch nor is it a fluffy purpose statement. It isn't a declaration or a statement of intent. It's a statement of fact. It explains in two or three short pithy sentences the SOI® at the core of your business in a way that any listener can immediately understand.

To be effective your positioning statement should be short, direct, inspiring, practical and absolutely genuine.

Short
People don't have the time nor the desire to listen to long-winded explanations. Keeping your statement down to two or three sentences will ensure it can be delivered in an elevator ride.

Direct
Don't beat about the bush. Your statement needs to be to the point, clear, concise, incisive and confident in tone.

Inspiring
You're not selling anything here but, without doubt, the explanation of why your business exists and how it is positioned to help society should be inspiring and meaningful. By the time I step out of that elevator, I want to feel like I have just met someone of significance who is making a difference in the world.

Practical
Your positioning statement replaces the need for old-fashioned, top-down generic vision and mission statements. Be practical and cut the clutter.

Genuine
A deeply embedded driver of change or superficial purpose wash? Your SOI® and values have been forged out of the truth of your business. It matters that your positioning statement is a sincere expression of fact that rings with the kind of candour that commands respect and demands serious contemplation.

Ultimately, your business will be judged on the things it does rather than the things it says. It's important, therefore, that your positioning statement guides and enables your business to do the right things.

Just like writing your values, getting your positioning statement right will take time and rehash after rehash. You'll know when you've cracked it – you will be surrounded by screwed up paper balls on the floor and a smile of achievement on your face.

Your positioning statement is based on your identified core values and SOI®. Weaving them together will help you form the two or three sentences you need to explain the value of your business.

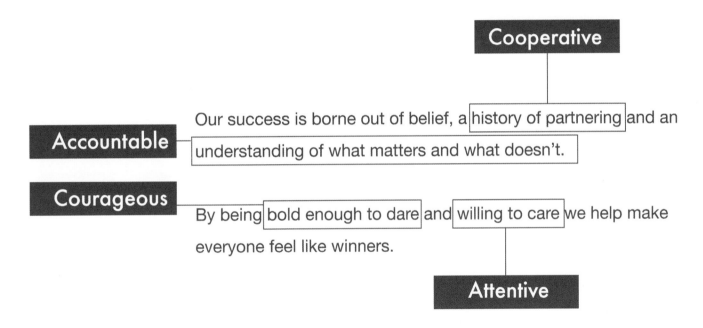

3.4 YOUR SINGLE ORGANIZING IDEA (SOI®)

The idea at the core of your business is the beating heart that pumps meaning and inspiration into every part of it. It's the central, unifying lodestar around which every decision, action, behaviour and communication is aligned.

Getting to your SOI® can be either easy or hard. Candidates may 'pop up' and even define themselves during the research phase as they did in this case: During the very final interview I conducted with a country director in Palestine, right at the very end of a long and rigorous research phase for an international NGO, she kept repeating to me the same phrase over and over again: "We are here for good". This was a particularly tense time in the region and it struck a chord with me and with my client back in Washington DC when I repeated it, and we quickly identified and defined 'Partners for Good' as an SOI® that could inspire, guide and drive the performance of every aspect of the organization.

On the other hand, defining an SOI® may take hours and hours, poring back and forth over

what you have found out, entering into extensive dialogue and brainstorming with your team to create a list that can be whittled down to a single powerful idea that has the potential to pass the stress test described overleaf.

The simplicity of an SOI® is deceptive; you need to have the courage to say less. It doesn't get any simpler than one word. 'Safety' has been Volvo's guiding star since 1927.

'Confidence' and 'pride' are two one-word SOI®s that are providing inspiration and daily guidance to two businesses I have worked with. Pride is the lodestar that motivates every aspect of the British fashion business Community Clothing. Pride runs through the roots and branches of the business. There is pride in the quality of design and craftsmanship, pride in the output figures achieved and targets reached, pride in the HR policies that give meaning and purpose to people living in disadvantaged areas, pride in bringing back to life factories that would otherwise lie dormant, and this pride is celebrated through shared successes. It's an idea that goes beyond the walls of the

business. People who wear the Community Clothing label feel pride in their choice.

The power of two or three worded SOI®s, such as 'Building Better Communities' and 'Collective Success', lies in the expression of both an outcome and a call to action. These two simply worded statements are calls to action that everyone finds easy to understand and to talk about.

Once you have your SOI®, values and positioning statement defined and written up, you have a:

1. Single: **one**
2. Organizing: **systematically coordinated**
3. Idea: **concept, that benefits all**

Now to test it!

Performance: A standard of success/achievement
Behaviour: Positive morals and ethics, kindness, fairness
Can be measured/assessed/factored

FEEL-GOOD

A human sense/emotion
Image: Quality, finish
Associated with aptitude, intuition, inclination
An outcome/reaction resulting from a
connection, experience (a moment of truth)

Your SOI® should be a call to action. The best SOI®s create
new efficiencies, deliver value to all your stakeholders, drive
performance, and generate a shared sense of achievement.
This example meets these criteria.

3.5 STRESS TESTING YOUR SOI®

Once you think you have created your SOI® Strategic Framework it's time to stress test it.

Set yourself and your team the task of considering the stress test questions set out here. Give them a few days to think about their answers alone and then bring them back together to discuss the short, medium and long-term implications and opportunities the strategic framework presents. Encourage them to think about your business in general and the function they look after in particular.

Remember what I said right at the beginning of this book: There is no such thing as a perfect strategy and there is no such thing as a perfect set of words. Consider this to be the ultimate question you will be asking yourself and your team: Will our chosen SOI® help our business to thrive commercially while contributing to making a positive difference in the world?

If the answer is yes, you can lock in your SOI® Strategic Framework and get on with making it a reality.

8 POINT STRESS TEST

Criterion 1:
Credible
Is the SOI® based on reality, hard facts and evidence?

Criterion 2:
Resilient
Will the SOI® be sustainable over the long-term regardless of management, technology and market changes?

Criterion 3:
Relevant
Will the SOI® deliver value to our business and our stakeholders?

Criterion 4:
Commercial
Will alignment with the SOI® help ensure that our business thrives and maintains commercial success?

Criterion 5:
Beneficial
Will the adoption of the SOI® impact positively on people and the planet?

Criterion 6:
SINGLE
Will the SOI® provide the single-minded focus required to help separate what is important from what is not?

Criterion 7:
ORGANIZING
Will each function of the business and the wider ecosystem be able to self-organize their alignment and contribution to the SOI®?

Criterion 8:
IDEA
Is the SOI® a compelling concept that people internally and externally will admire and aspire to be a part of?

Moments of truth in our value chain. At a glance, how good (or bad) do we feel about our choices, practices and policies?							
Design	Raw materials	Fabric & yarn production	Garment production	Transport	Sales	Customers	Recycling
Choice of materials: Looks Style Quality	Processing of raw materials: Working conditions (time, safety, health, wages) Water usage Chemical usage	Production of yarn and fabrics in mills: Working conditions (time, safety, health, wages), Water usage, Chemical usage, Greenhouse gas emissions	In our own factories, as well as our suppliers: Working conditions (time, safety, health, wages) Environmental standards	Transportation from factories to distribution and sales outlets: Greenhouse gas emissions Transport types Transport distance	Selling products: Working conditions and environments of outlet Energy usage of stores, offices and warehouses. Data privacy for colleagues and customers, Responsible advertising Fast fashion versus sustainable fashion	Care for clothes at home: Energy usage/ greenhouse emissions Water usage Microfibre contamination Detergent usage	Garment after use: Collection Repurposing Recycling Reprocessing fibres
Feel-good?	Feel-good?	Feel-good?	Feel-good?	Feel-good?	Feel-good?	Feel-good?	Feel-good?

Prove it! It's all well and good having the intent but the bottom line is delivering real action. Will acting on your SOI® drive new efficiencies into the value chain, help reconcile product offers, and make better use of the ecosystem that surrounds your business? Will your SOI® make your business a better business and the world a better place and can you measure it to prove the impact that you are having? In this SOI® example, feel-good is a factor that can be measured and improved upon.

KEY POINTS

 Your SOI® Strategic Framework brings together your positioning statement, values and SOI® to succinctly explain the **why**, **what** and **how** of your business.

 Your core values are defined to become bedrock realities that are put to use every day to deliver positive, commercial performance results.

 Your positioning statement must be a sincere expression of fact that rings with the kind of candour that commands respect and demands serious contemplation.

 Your SOI® is the guiding star around which every decision and action is aligned. Everyone who knows your business knows they will find you there. The simpler the better: you need to have the courage to say less.

 The moment of truth: stress test your chosen SOI® to ensure it will advance your business and contribute to making a positive difference in the world. Once it's passed the test, it's locked in!

YOUR NOTES

SOI™

SINGLE

ORGANIZING

IDEA

4.0   59-84

ALIGN

How to implement your SOI® These tools will
help you align with your SOI® and start making a
difference to your business performance and society.

4.1 TOTAL ALIGNMENT

"The future is here – it's just not evenly distributed." So said the science fiction writer William Gibson. Right now your SOI® is just words on a page, but what your business and the world needs is action. Alignment of your entire business with your SOI® is an ideal to be met and an objective to be achieved. To ensure your SOI® isn't seen as a work of fiction you need to turn it into fact. But change takes time and, as the quote implies, it doesn't all arrive at the same time.

While the SOI® will provide the focal point for your business going forward, it will take time for its benefits to be fully understood and realised. Think of alignment as each part of your business setting out on a journey (see diagram opposite). Some parts may have short journeys and can move along them relatively quickly, while other parts struggle to overcome challenges and obstacles that stand in the way.

Potential and evolution, not revolution, needs to be the key message, especially if your business is based on the traditional top-down model.

Inevitably for some, carrying on with the old way of doing things is much easier than reaching for the stars, especially if the point of doing so is not immediately clear. Culture, morale, resources, commitments, calendars, relationships, organizational structure, processes, practices and understanding, among many other factors, will all play a role in dictating the pace of change and the evenness of it across your business.

You shouldn't think of the approach to aligning with an SOI® as a sequential process that is set at one pace. Instead, you should view it as an ongoing constant that relies upon different levels of commitment and action at different times from different parts of your business. It is like moving up a staircase of steps of varying heights along a line of upward progress.

Implementation is rarely straightforward, and, in my experience, never complete. The principles of continuous improvement (Kaizen) play a substantial role in affecting the change associated with the adoption and embedding of an SOI®.

The process of creating your SOI® in the identify and define phases has brought your business together very quickly to solve a set challenge. This newfound sense of achievement through collaboration is the key to solving how your business transitions to alignment with your SOI® as you progress. Applying the skills, expertise and intelligence of the people in and around your business will not only further cement them around a common cause but simultaneously produce tangible outcomes that create new efficiencies and new opportunities that benefit everyone.

You've set the foundation for your business, and created momentum. Now it's time to take action. This part of the book is dedicated to explaining exactly how you do that.

Communicated position
Do internal and external communications consistently express and support the SOI® through media channels? Are service/product experiences, impacts and innovations advancing the enterprise towards the SOI®?

Stories & experiences

Ideal position
Is the enterprise positioned for future success around an SOI® that is embedded at the core of the business which will deliver sustainable business and societal benefits?

SOI®

Culture & behaviour

Actual position
Does the root and branch reality of the structure, culture and behaviour of people in the enterprise align with values that are moving it towards the SOI®?

Leadership

Word of mouth

Conceived position
Do perceptions of the organization, its image, behaviour and performance, consistently align with a sustainable purpose that external stakeholders understand, buy into and actively contribute to?

Desired position
Is leadership totally committed? Does leadership consistently plan, reference, measure and promote the value of the SOI® through statements, speeches, discussions, reports, decisions and commitments?

Inspired by Professor John Balmer's ACCID test

Reaching for the star All businesses are different, but the length of the dotted lines on this graphic indicate elements of your business that you can expect to align first and what parts will take longer.

4.2 BUSINESS FUNCTIONS

If you have led and resourced your business to enable it to go through the identify and define phases of the SOI® process you have completed the first task of any leader, which is to provide the tools and mechanisms required to reach a shared vision of the future that benefits all. The next task is to help the functions of your business come together and make that vision a reality, progressing your business from what it is today to what it will become in the future.

Look up the key functions or activities of any business on the internet and you will find a wide range of lists. Most will include sales, marketing, production, operations, IT, HR, finance, accounting and management. None will include 'doing good'. This is the status quo.

SOI® makes doing good the key role of business and challenges the status quo by enabling the holistic alignment of functions to achieve that outcome. In traditional businesses the pursuit of the activities listed above are carried out by separate departments (some outsourced). This separation fuels silo thinking, gives rise to rivalries, promotes unnecessary internal competition, creates confusion, undermines reliability and destroys any chance of unity. Rethinking the functions of your business to create a more holistic structure that is aligned with your SOI®, the no.1 priority, will help mitigate workplace stress, break down barriers, and deliver the many rewards of shared success.

Cooperation and collaboration gives root to the SOI®. This means giving the functions of your business the time, responsibility, resources and tools to adjust to and carry out the work required to achieve alignment with it.

The tools are described on the following pages. The management, finance and accounting create the conditions that allow this to happen are provided by you specifically by:

1. Encouraging and making possible alignment with the SOI® by providing the training, development and resources needed to allow the different parts of your business to respond to the changes that alignment will demand.

2. Exemplify the SOI® and values that underpin it. (See more on leadership in the next section).

3. Monitor, judge, set standards and objectives against which the performance of your business can be measured and accountability appraised.

4. Consistently convey and reinforce the direction of travel through stakeholder communications.

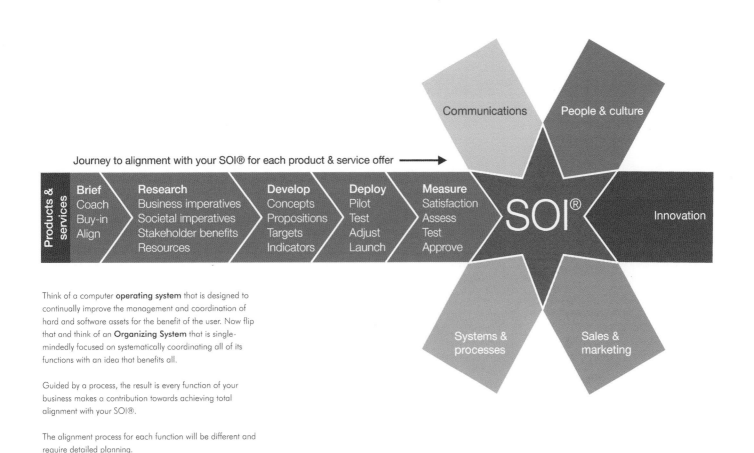

Journey to alignment with your SOI® for each product & service offer →

Products & services

Brief
Coach
Buy-in
Align

Research
Business imperatives
Societal imperatives
Stakeholder benefits
Resources

Develop
Concepts
Propositions
Targets
Indicators

Deploy
Pilot
Test
Adjust
Launch

Measure
Satisfaction
Assess
Test
Approve

SOI®

Communications

People & culture

Innovation

Systems & processes

Sales & marketing

Think of a computer **operating system** that is designed to continually improve the management and coordination of hard and software assets for the benefit of the user. Now flip that and think of an **Organizing System** that is single-mindedly focused on systematically coordinating all of its functions with an idea that benefits all.

Guided by a process, the result is every function of your business makes a contribution towards achieving total alignment with your SOI®.

The alignment process for each function will be different and require detailed planning.

4.2/1 PEOPLE & CULTURE

"Culture eats strategy for breakfast," said management guru Peter Drucker. It's true, so the first thing you need to do to ensure your culture won't get in the way of delivering on the strategy is to make certain everyone is on board.

I'll be clear and say this is not easy – but you do have a head start, because from the outset you have involved everyone in the identification and definition of the values and SOI®, and you will have created some goodwill and addressed some of the cynicism that comes with change.

The idea of making a contribution that makes a difference to the world and people's lives is a powerful one. Most people want to do just that and if you give them the opportunity and the mechanisms they will. You only have to recall the astonishing acts carried out during the COVID-19 crisis. Nevertheless, it will be tough. At the end of one project I led, after the senior management team had stressed tested and agreed the strategic framework, it was obvious that one member was not on board. It was tough, as he was a high-performing individual but a spectator (see diagram across). It was the

right decision to let him go and that is exactly what the CEO did, guided by the greater good that the SOI® and the values would bring. This was the first act where leadership and strategy combined to deliver a decision, and it sent a clear signal through the business that underlined the importance of the SOI®.

Stepping off
There are lots of different ways to introduce both your SOI® strategic framework and what it will mean for your business in the future. If you run a small business in one location then gathering everyone together on a special day that has some sort of significance to your business is a good idea. If your business is spread over multiple locations, a roadshow is a perfect solution. Whichever way you decide to reveal your SOI® and the future direction, your presentation should feel like an event that includes:

1. Why being a force for good is necessary.

2. Exactly how the SOI®, values and positioning statement were arrived at.

3. What will be happening in the short and medium term to turn words into actions.

4. Recognition and celebration of the milestone that has already been achieved.

Your audience should leave feeling that they are no longer just doing a job but are contributing to a greater cause that will fulfil them as individuals, change the business they work for, for good, and benefit the world around them.

Humanising business
Inevitably, the strategic framework is being presented from the top down so it is very important that emphasis is put on the collaboration that was required to identify and define the SOI®. This needs to be underlined at every opportunity, as does the empathy and camaraderie that was tapped into in order to create the solution. Aligning with the SOI® will bring about system and operational changes that will humanise your business in a way that will give freedom to the people within it to achieve and celebrate new definitions of success.

Spectators

% of total employees

These individuals are self-centred. They understand the aims of the organization but have elected not to take part for personal reasons. They can often be quite senior.

Stars

% of total employees

These individuals are highly involved on both levels. They understand the big picture, actively participate and encourage others to take part.

Seekers

% of total employees

These individuals have plans outside of the organization. They do not believe the company can help them realise their dreams or goals.

Settlers

% of total employees

The organization meets the expectations of these content individuals. But they don't have the understanding or tools they need to contribute more to it beyond their daily roles.

HIGH — Understanding — LOW

LOW — Commitment — HIGH

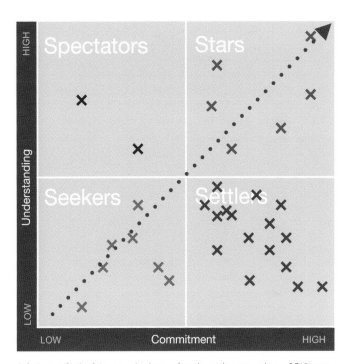

HIGH — Understanding — LOW

LOW — Commitment — HIGH

Spectators | Stars
Seekers | Settlers

Settlers to Stars Businesses where staff have a clear understanding of an objective that they care about and have the tools needed to help achieve that objective out-perform those that don't. Successful alignment with your SOI® empowers employees, giving them a sense of personal fulfilment and shared purpose. For the business, it enhances levels of performance, increases employee retention figures and, ultimately, delivers better stakeholder experiences.

Who's contributing? Assessing the degree of employee alignment with your SOI® goes beyond traditional HR filters. Its objective is to quantify the degree to which the role of the employee impacts on delivering outcomes that align with and underpin the SOI®.

4.2/1 PEOPLE & CULTURE (cont.)

Understanding the value of values

The values, customs, beliefs and behaviours of people is the number one determining factor dictating how successful alignment will be. Simply put, alignment with your SOI® across the functions of your business will be limited unless everyone understands the importance and role of your core values. A good way to do that is first to get everyone on the same piece of paper when it comes to understanding how values influence the decisions we make and what gets done in our personal lives. This short one-hour workshop, with the aid of the workbook illustrated opposite, will help with that process.

Step 1

Working in pairs

1. Participants start the process by asking their opposite number, "What do you feel are the most important values to you personally?"
2. Each value and the meaning behind them is written down using the exact words spoken (because different words mean different things to different people), in the meaning/belief space provided.
3. The list is confirmed and the roles swapped.

Step 2

With the lists of both people completed the participants are asked to rank their values on their own.

1. What values are always important and what values are sometimes important?
2. Values with the same sort of meaning should be amalgamated so that a list of no more than five values is arrived at.

Step 3

Having established that values influence the decisions that people make and that they have varying degrees of importance, the final step is to bring the entire group together to complete the workbook by discussing how personal values will help reinforce the values of your business.

By making a version of this values exercise part of recruiting you can both attract the right people and foreground your commitment to your SOI® at an early stage.

Living and breathing it

Your core values are a critical part of the SOI® system and not decoration for your walls.

Putting it bluntly, they need to be imposed and constantly monitored, ensuring everyone is acting in line with them. Employee performance, hiring and firing procedures, recognition and promotion policies should all be informed by your core values. Carefully explained and woven into every aspect of your business, your values together with your SOI®, will create a sense of unity, underpin standards and humanise your business in a way that appeals to hearts as well as minds.

Standing together

Leadership is an action, not a post; standing up for your core values and SOI® should be an expectation of everyone. However, even in the flattest of organizations, people in different positions clearly have different opportunities to influence progress. Their efforts should be recognised.

As a general guide:

Those in leadership should be recognised for:

• **Convincing** stakeholders (internal and external) that the SOI® can be relied upon to deliver benefits for all stakeholders.

- Establishing, driving and directing transformation initiatives.
- Motivating and inspiring by 'walking the talk'.

Those in management posts should be recognised for:
- **Organizing** and managing alignment efforts.
- Encouraging collaboration and positive contributions.
- Encouraging a shared culture of success.

Staff grades should be recognised for:
- **Participating** in alignment efforts.
- Providing feedback.

Celebration

Note that I say recognition and not reward. Doing the right thing doesn't necessarily need to be rewarded. But it should always be recognised. Bringing your business together to celebrate passing milestones on your journey to being a business for good will be energised by turning shared successes into shared pride.

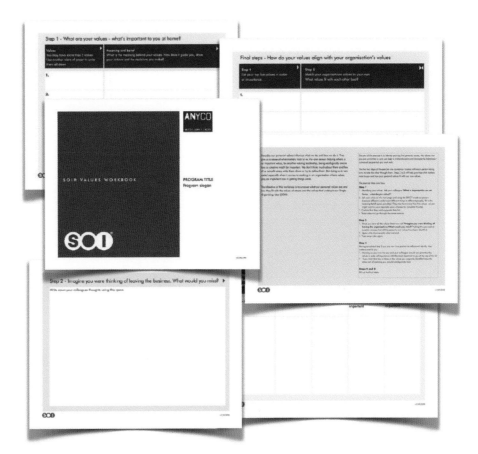

4.2/2 INNOVATION

Very few businesses run innovation programs that involve their staff and stakeholders in the development of fresh ideas. Businesses may conduct product and service-related R&D (research and development), but this is not the same as creating a mechanism that will nurture and incubate ideas that engage and improve the whole of your business, its value chain, and the ecosystem beyond.

With an SOI® at the core of your business that staff and stakeholders not only understand but also helped define, a unique opportunity exists to build on the momentum and collaboration that has been generated to start new initiatives, stop old inefficiencies, and identify current activity that already aligns with your SOI®.

As soon as your SOI® is validated you can use it to challenge staff and stakeholders to create an innovation programme such as the one illustrated opposite. Dedicating time and effort to bring your SOI® to life through a bespoke innovation program that you can brand with a name and slogan related to your SOI® will not only enable you to tap into the collective wisdom of your stakeholders but also provide a very practical means to regularly deliver new ideas that will solve real-world problems.

Such an innovation program will create vibrant forums within your business, empower people to create links to networks and partners externally, generate stories, create momentum, as well as reap the rewards of continual improvement. By regularly communicating and recognising the progress of innovations that are in development and being delivered, you will send a clear signal of your commitment to seeking a better way and clarify that this is part and parcel of the day-to-day life of your business, not just a reputation building one-off stunt.

The SOI® innovation program illustrated and explained overleaf is a framework that you should adapt to suit your own needs. Toyota famously made innovation everyone's business with its 'Always a Better Way' program that empowers individuals to make suggestions that maximise quality, minimise waste and improve efficiencies. Google is similarly famous for enabling all of its people to contribute ideas through its '70-20-10 policy' which stipulates that 70% of an employee's time should be spent on core duties, 20% on activities that advance the business, and 10% on activities that advance the individual. The result is not only a flow of new thinking aligned with Google's core idea of 'universal accessibility', but a dynamic culture that thrives and takes pride in its ability to continually move forward and break new ground. In a nutshell, creating an innovation program that benefits both your business and society will stimulate, motivate and make your business more dynamic. Beyond those outcomes, delivering new ideas that solve real problems will earn the trust, advocacy and loyalty of your stakeholders.

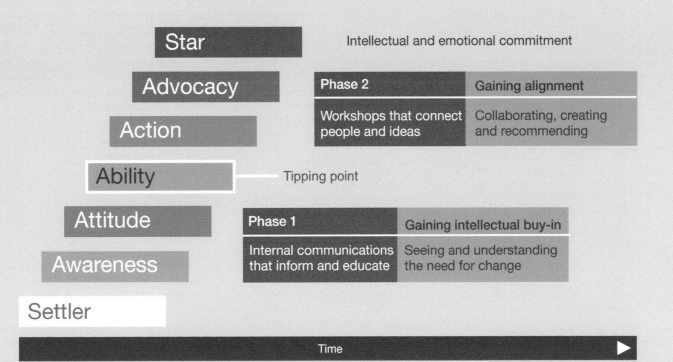

Star

Intellectual and emotional commitment

Advocacy

Phase 2	Gaining alignment
Workshops that connect people and ideas	Collaborating, creating and recommending

Action

Ability — Tipping point

Attitude

Phase 1	Gaining intellectual buy-in
Internal communications that inform and educate	Seeing and understanding the need for change

Awareness

Settler

Time ▶

Tipping point SOI® encourages a culture of collaboration and innovation that, in turn, generates ideas that make things better for all involved. Getting to the high-performance culture this creates is a journey that takes practical plans, time and leadership.

4.2/2 INNOVATION (cont.)

Innovation program

The objective of the innovation program is to generate new ideas and efficiencies that will deliver sustainable benefits to your business and beyond in a manageable way.

All your staff should participate in the innovation workshops. The program will spread knowledge, encourage collaboration and, for many, provide an opportunity for personal achievement. But, as with all change, it will require communications that encourage participation and time to allow people to adjust.

Making real the ideas collected from your workshops will be the clearest indication of your commitment to your SOI® and its potential to deliver positive changes. New ideas will enhance the reputation of your business amongst your key stakeholders, improve the efficiency of your business, and provide a mechanism for sharing and celebrating the success of your strategy. It will also allow you to monitor and measure the level of understanding and commitment to the SOI® within your business, and where there are strengths and weaknesses.

The program is divided into three phases. How long your business takes to complete them depends on the resources you have available.

Phase 1

Held throughout your business within a set period of time, the workshops should be facilitated by 'Stars' (see chapter on people and culture) in the business who have been briefed on the program. They will take staff through three exercises to complete a workbook:

Exercise 1: Story harvest

This simple exercise encourages participants to share existing examples of your values and SOI® at work in your business today. Recorded by the facilitator, these stories can be curated and later brought to life and shared internally and externally to demonstrate how and where your business is making a difference.

Exercise 2: Touch-points

Some of your staff may already be familiar with touch-points if they contributed to the research phase of identifying your SOI®. In this exercise participants are first asked to work

together to identify all the touch-points in their part of the business and then to select the top five where they feel that change needs to be prioritised.

Exercise 3: Start-stop-keep

Reviewing each of the five selected touch-points in turn, participants are asked to recommend what your business should:

- **Start** doing at that touch-point
- **Stop** doing at that touch-point
- **Keep** doing that already supports the SOI®

Phase 2

Once completed, the workbooks are sent to be assessed by your SOI® core team and a plan created that details what actions should be taken by who and when (see the SOI® Alignment Canvas on page 81).

Phase 3

The final phase of the process celebrates the new ideas by sharing news on their impact and recognising the contributions made by your staff to making them real.

SOI® Innovation program

PHASE 1	PHASE 2	PHASE 3
SOI® INNOVATION WORKSHOPS	**SOI® WORKING GROUP**	**SOI® STAKEHOLDERS**
CROWDSOURCING	ASSESSING	EXECUTING
Story and insight gathering Touchpoint identification/prioritisation Start_Stop_Keep ideas	Submission review (Criteria) Action selection Action planning (Who, how, where, when)	Action implementation Celebration/recognition

RECOMMENDATIONS → **ASSESSMENT** | **SELECTION** | **PLANNING** → **IMPLEMENTATION**

| JAN | FEB | MAR | APR | MAY | JUN | JUL | AUG | SEP | OCT | NOV | DEC |

Ongoing stakeholder communication and collaboration ▶

Controlled, continual adaption New ideas drive sustainable progress, create a buzz and bring momentum that, in turn, results in the generation of greater participation and more ideas. The innovation program and workbook referred to here provide a controlled and manageable system that can be adapted to suit your business, its resources and calendar of events.

4.2/3 PRODUCTS & SERVICES

Ultimately, the success of your business depends on the level of satisfaction that your customers gain from using the products and services you sell. Offering products and service that are fit for the future is what alignment with an SOI® is all about. You may have products and services which simply don't fit with your SOI®. These will undoubtedly provide important income streams, but this is where the rubber hits the road. Ceasing to supply products and services that are not sustainable will speak volumes about you and your business; committing to developing and delivering new ones will crank that volume up even more.

Better by design
I studied design at university and ran a successful design consultancy in London for almost 10 years. Design and the process of designing has influenced my entire life. Specifically, simplicity has been a design quality that I have always admired and sought after. It has been my long-held belief that keeping things simple and avoiding complexity leads to a kind of purity and authenticity that delivers better outcomes and superior levels of satisfaction.

The idea that 'less is better' could not be more relevant to any business today; nor could the 10 principles that the celebrated German product designer Dieter Rams introduced to the world. Sustainable product development and '**Good Design**' (or design for good) he said:

1. **Is innovative** – The possibilities for progression are not, by any means, exhausted. Technological development is always offering new opportunities for original designs. But imaginative design always develops in tandem with improving technology, and can never be an end in itself.

2. **Makes a product useful** – A product is bought to be used. It has to satisfy not only functional, but also psychological and aesthetic criteria. Good design emphasises the usefulness of a product whilst disregarding anything that could detract from it.

3. **Is aesthetic** – The aesthetic quality of a product is integral to its usefulness because products are used every day and have an effect on people and their well-being. Only well-executed objects can be beautiful.

4. **Makes a product understandable** – It clarifies the product's structure. Better still, it can make the product clearly express its function by making use of the user's intuition. It's self-explanatory.

5. **Is unobtrusive** – Products fulfilling a purpose are like tools. They are neither decorative objects nor works of art. Their design should, therefore, be both neutral and restrained, to leave room for the user's self-expression.

6. **Is honest** – It does not make a product appear more innovative, powerful or valuable than it really is. It does not attempt to manipulate the consumer with promises that cannot be kept.

7. **Is long-lasting** – It avoids being fashionable and therefore never appears

antiquated. Unlike fashionable design, it lasts many years – even in today's throwaway society.

8. **Is thorough down to the last detail** – Nothing must be arbitrary or left to chance. Care and accuracy in the design process show respect towards the consumer.

9. **Is environmentally friendly** – Design makes an important contribution to the preservation of the environment. It conserves resources and minimises physical and visual pollution throughout the lifecycle of the product.

10. **Is minimal** – Less is more. Simple as possible but not simpler. Good design elevates the essential functions of a product.

Guided by your SOI®, Dieter's principles together with industry standards, such as ISO, IIP or ERM, will help you ensure your products and services appeal to the growing numbers of customers, workers and investors who want to support businesses that simultaneously improve their lives while benefiting society and the environment.

Alignment in action

Alignment with your SOI® provides a disciplined approach to reviewing and improving the appeal, efficiency and sustainability of your products and services through the phases briefly described here:

Phase 1 Introduce

The first phase is geared towards ensuring the people involved in product and service development are thoroughly immersed in the SOI® strategic framework and understand its purpose as the reference point against which product and service development is conducted.

Phase 2 Research

Consumer preferences and market opportunities are evaluated and product/service requirements are defined. Resources are identified and execution plans for a successful program launch are developed.

Phase 3 Develop

During the product development phase models are built, concepts are assessed, and social and environmental standards are identified and ratified. A clear explanation of what the service or product does and how it aligns with your SOI® is drafted.

Phase 4 Deploy

Once a prototype product or pilot service has passed testing through a quality control process (internal and/or external), the product or service can be commercially launched for general availability.

Phase 5 Measure

Experiences should be monitored and feedback used to improve your product or service offer in alignment with your SOI®. Gathering this knowledge can be helpful in understanding the life cycle of your products and the learnings applied to future product and service offers.

4.2/4 COMMUNICATION

It is important that all your stakeholders and especially your employees understand that your SOI® is critical to the future success of your business.

The positive changes that an SOI® will bring to your business will be considerable and will need to be clearly signalled. But tread carefully. Caution and complete transparency should be the watchwords concerning all messages related to your SOI®. How, when and where the messages are delivered needs to be thoroughly thought through and risk assessed. A stage-gate communications plan should be prepared to ensure the language that is used to support the establishment of your SOI® at the core of your business doesn't get dismissed as a slick marketing campaign.

The trick is to recognise that there is a gap between aspiration and reality. To bridge that gap initial communications should simply underline the importance and value of your SOI® and include invitations to contribute to it rather than declaring its potential to save the world.

The problem with BP's infamous strap-line to go "Beyond Petroleum" was that only some of parts of the business were actually doing so or intended to do so. In his 2015 book *Connect: How Companies Succeed by Radically Engaging Society*, CEO and architect of the vision, Lord John Browne says that what he deeply regrets more than anything was the failure to manage the gap between aspiration and reality. In other words, the rhetoric didn't line up with what was actually happening. The advertising agency involved probably wouldn't have liked the lack of slickness and neat fit with the BP name, but "Going Beyond Petroleum" rather than "Beyond Petroleum" would have been more open, accurate and less incendiary.

In my experience, advertising and PR agencies, in particular, need to be extremely carefully managed and strictly guided to ensure that passionate but misguided creativity and short-term financial gain do not generate unintentional consequences. A damaged reputation will undermine all the work you have done to identify, define and implement your SOI®.

Announcing goals related to your SOI® and regularly reporting on progress is a smart way to manage communications and will provide the basis for an ongoing dialogue that takes your audiences on a journey with you. Opening this two-way dialogue and creating a sense of shared journey with your stakeholders through communications will not only build trust and enhance the reputation of your business, it will help you better understand priorities and identify changes that drive even better performance.

Your website, product and service labelling, social media channels, events and annual reports are all useful channels through which to publish your achievements and the data that back them up.

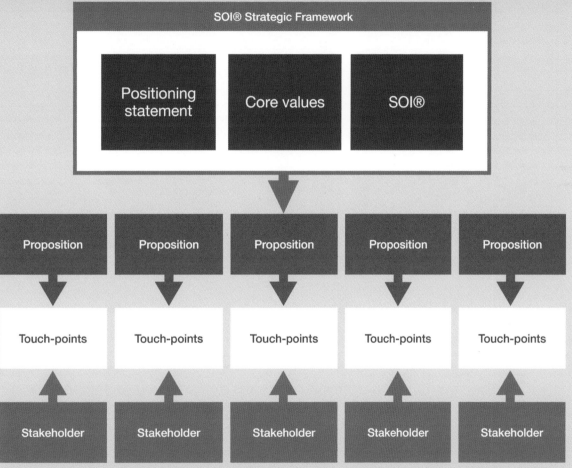

SOI® Strategic Framework

Positioning statement | Core values | SOI®

Proposition | Proposition | Proposition | Proposition | Proposition

Touch-points | Touch-points | Touch-points | Touch-points | Touch-points

Stakeholder | Stakeholder | Stakeholder | Stakeholder | Stakeholder

Clarity, consistency and character Successes resulting from your SOI® will bring substance to your messages and enhance the value propositions you present to your stakeholder audiences. A disciplined approach that always refers back to your SOI® will also ensure clarity and consistency at key touch-points.

4.2/5 SALES & MARKETING

Your marketing strategies and how you sell your products and services will need to be reviewed and revised to align with your SOI®.

Just like your competitors, it is highly likely your business has reacted to and been largely defined by the market and what it wants – chasing the dollar. Market demands don't just trigger isolated marketing initiatives, they can lead to all sorts of knee-jerk reactions from continually reframing value propositions to developing sub brands and even rushing to produce previously unplanned product and service offers. That the sales and marketing function has such a dominant and leading role is a major problem for many businesses as they struggle to adapt continually to the ever-changing trends and whims of the market.

In the face of this continual onslaught, spurred by a war of attrition with competitors, the de facto advice is often 'adapt or die'. Sales and marketing and all that follows is, for most, **reactive**. But remember the stress testing criteria? Your SOI® was specifically chosen

precisely because it would be sustainable and relevant "regardless of technology, management and market" changes. In a nutshell, your SOI® is grounded in a **proactive** long-term strategy that we know appeals to a growing segment of the market.

The fact the whole of your business, and not just the marketing department, is committed to and organized around a single strategy that caters for a very clearly defined customer type ensures the balance is maintained and marketing isn't leading – your SOI® is.

The focus your SOI® brings means that research, including market research, can be more targeted and precise in its design and application, as well as more cost-effective – which is another plus. No longer do you need to invest in ill-focused market research that is often so vast it escapes any possibility of practical application.

Armed with precise research and a detailed understanding of your customers, your brand marketing slogans, symbols and key messages

can be better crafted to appeal to their specific needs, wants and values. In addition, routes to market, whether they be person-to-person, online or through sales correspondence, can be carefully tailored to ensure these moments of truth are aligned with your SOI® and your values.

Single-minded focus on your SOI®, coupled with a detailed knowledge of your customer base, means the initial selling approaches and customer relationship management (CRM) will be backed up by the whole of your business and not just marketing fluff. Outstanding CRM depends on ensuring that the entirety of your business is aligned with your SOI®, and marketing promises are backed up and grounded in product and service offers which deliver what is expected of a business that has positioned itself as a force for good.

Monitoring your performance through regular surveys and other feedback mechanisms will create opportunities to further your business, demonstrate your difference, and the difference your business makes.

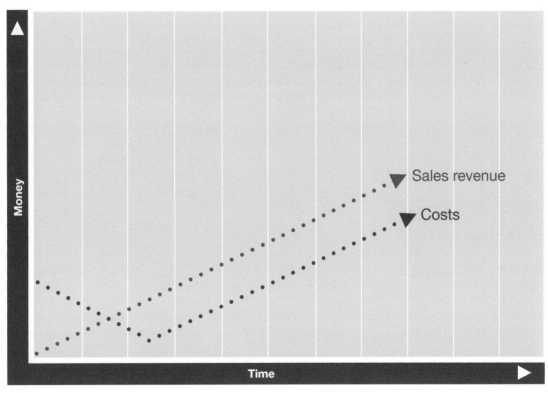

Lets thrive This is the simplest graphic in the whole book. Your business needs to be profitable to cover its costs and some. The some (or profit) is what you use to prepare for and invest in the future. You need to make a profit if you are going to make a difference. The objective is not to maximise profit, however, it is to maintain the profitability required to thrive and deliver your SOI® related objectives.

4.2/6 PROCESSES & SYSTEMS

Your processes and systems impact every aspect of your business – productivity, innovation, marketing, human and financial resources.

Having a defined SOI® enables you to organize and set clear objectives that focus your processes and systems in a way that converts internal costs, time, effort and resources into external results.

Translating your SOI® into clear objectives that govern and guide the processes and systems you use to get things done ensures you are sufficiently organized to turn the good intention that your SOI® stands for into a reality. Setting goals or objectives is the only method that can concentrate people's efforts and your resources on running your business and delivering real change on a day-to-day basis. Without objectives your SOI® Strategic Framework will be simply remembered as an interesting exercise that resulted in little more than a set of words that sounded good but delivered nothing.

A systematic analysis of your processes, systems, policies and standards will help identify what fits with your SOI® and what doesn't. Taking your business with you on a journey to define and identify an SOI® is not without its challenges, and you can expect the same pain and difficulties when you come to overhauling, and perhaps even abandoning altogether, long-held processes and systems that have not been questioned before.

The objectives you set should be regarded and understood as standards against which performance can be measured and progress reported. They should motivate rather than dictate. Like your core values, the objectives you set are commitments. The right set will determine the structure of your business and how things get done; but they are not outcomes in themselves, just the means to achieve an outcome: alignment with your SOI® and the difference the journey towards it will make.

You have one SOI® but to achieve it you can expect there to be multiple objectives governing the processes and systems across all the different parts of your business. These help make people make the right choices, raise standards, enhance efficiency and drive performance.

The objectives you set should be easily understood and feel like common sense. They need to be clear, unambiguous, motivational and set against deadlines, and their achievement should be made accountable.

The more efficiently you run your business the greater your contribution to society will be. Great businesses are built when internal actions result in consistent delivery on external promises. Objectives will ensure the processes and systems you employ turn an intangible promise into a tangible reality.

SOI® Reward and recognition scheme

Innovation awards	Culture awards	Community awards
Staff teams recognised and rewarded for **start-stop-keep** ideas that support your SOI®	Individuals recognised and rewarded for actions/behaviours aligned with the **values** that support your SOI®	External ecosystem **partners/partnerships** recognised and rewarded for start-stop-keep ideas that align with your SOI®
Awarded annually Judgement by leadership Managed by peer elected team	Awarded annually/monthly Judgement by peers and leadership Managed by elected working group	Awarded annually Judgement by leadership Managed by elected working group
Reward value/type Rankings/categories	Reward value/type Rankings/categories	Reward value/type Rankings/categories
Assessment criteria Alignment with SOI® Potential impact Return on investment (ROI) Implementation speed	Assessment criteria Alignment with values Impact of actions/behaviour	Assessment criteria Alignment with SOI® Potential impact
Communications Pre-award campaign Award publicity Post-award publicity	Communications Pre-award campaign Award publicity Post-award publicity	Communications Pre-award campaign Award publicity Post-award publicity

Event(s) responsibility, planning, management and costing

Recognising performance that makes a difference Reward and recognition schemes create a sense of shared pride in your staff, they help retain key people and can attract high performers. The advantage of a scheme linked to an SOI®, such as the one illustrated here, is the motivation behind the scheme is beneficial not just to your business but also to the individuals and ecosystem partners who take part in it.

4.3 SOI® ALIGNMENT CANVAS

The SOI® alignment canvas is a template that captures exactly how and when you are going to turn ideas into realties that will make a difference to your business and stakeholders. It's a visual chart describing all the alignment commitments your business and its individual functions are planning to carry out over the short, medium and long term.

Printed out on a large laminated surface, it is a practical, hands-on tool to gather your team around and use post-it notes, stickers and marker pens to discuss and plan what alignment with your SOI® looks like.

Think of the canvas like this: If your SOI® is the guiding star upon which you have set the direction of your business, then the SOI® Alignment Canvas is the map showing you and your stakeholders how to get there – at a glance.

Making your SOI® Alignment Canvas a living document will require you to regularly update and refine the information on it. Like all plans it needs to evolve as your idea of what a future based on thriving looks like.

The SOI® Alignment canvas is made up of three blocks of information:

1. Your SOI® Strategic Framework
2. Your business function commitments
3. Your goals and resources at a glance

1. SOI® Strategic Framework
On the left-hand side of the canvas are the three, locked-in elements, that are guiding all your decision making: Your SOI®, your values and your positioning statement.

2. Business function commitments
The largest part of the canvas is given over to your business functions. From the innovation program you run you will receive input from each business function. This input answers the basic question, "If we are to align our part of the business with our Single Organizing Idea, what should we start, stop or keep doing?" The answer to that question will generate a longlist of ideas from which a filtered shortlist of commitments can be selected and prioritised for delivery over the short, medium and long term.

3. Goals and resources at a glance
On the right of the canvas is the final list of commitments that you have selected to become goals for your business over the long, medium and short term. Also logged here are the estimated costs, responsibility and deadline for each commitment.

Further down there's a space to summarise the overall costs for each term, and below that a space to list the key partnerships in your ecosystem you have identified who you will need to work with to achieve your goals.

A resource box summarises what human, physical and intellectual assets will be required. The canvas is your overall plan at a glance. The fine detail should be captured in a supporting document. Like all the tools in this Playbook you can adapt and customise the template to suit your needs.

SOI® Alignment Canvas

	Date/version

SOI® Strategic Framework

Business function commitments

Goals and resources

SOI®

Positioning statement

Core values

PEOPLE & CULTURE

ACTION	IDEAS			
START				
STOP				
KEEP				

INNOVATION

ACTION	IDEAS			
START				
STOP				
KEEP				

PRODUCTS & SERVICES

ACTION	IDEAS			
START				
STOP				
KEEP				

COMMUNICATIONS

ACTION	IDEAS			
START				
STOP				
KEEP				

SALES & MARKETING

ACTION	IDEAS			
START				
STOP				
KEEP				

PROCESSES & SYSTEMS

ACTION	IDEAS			
START				
STOP				
KEEP				

Short term goals

Medium term goals

Long term goals

Cost summary

Resources

Ecosystem partnerships

KEY POINTS

 Your business and the world needs action. Implementing your SOI® turns good intentions into actions by systematically coordinating all your business functions with it.

 It will take time, effort and patience to align, but the process will unleash new opportunities and new levels of commitment from staff, customers, and investors who see the benefits for themselves.

 A business-wide search for innovations related to your SOI® will further stimulate colleagues – and earn the trust, advocacy and loyalty of all your stakeholders.

 Stopping unsustainable products and services will speak volumes about you and your business. Committing to developing new ones will crank up that volume even more.

 Announcing goals related to your SOI® and reporting on progress is a smart way to manage communications and will help you take your stakeholders on the journey with you.

YOUR NOTES

SINGLE

ORGANIZING

IDEA

5.0

MEASURE

How you measure the impact of your SOI® These tools will help you understand the difference your business is making in real time.

5.1 SOI® LEARNING LOOPS

How do you know your SOI® is generating commercial and social value? Is it working as expected? What is its impact? The best way to answer these questions is to measure alignment together with your stakeholders.

Creating an SOI® Learning Loop with each of your stakeholder groups will give you access to a drumbeat of metrics, reflections and actions that will help you understand the relevance and momentum your SOI® is generating. Inviting your staff and external constituents to pick up and follow the scent will help to ensure your SOI® is on track and contributing to a better business and a better world.

In the early days of your SOI® engaging your stakeholders in frequent surveys and measurement activities will create a virtuous cycle of knowledge and participation which, in turn, will build alignment and generate momentum behind your SOI®. With understanding comes awareness, and – if your SOI® is meeting your stakeholders' expectations and values – increased engagement with your cause, and loyalty to your business.

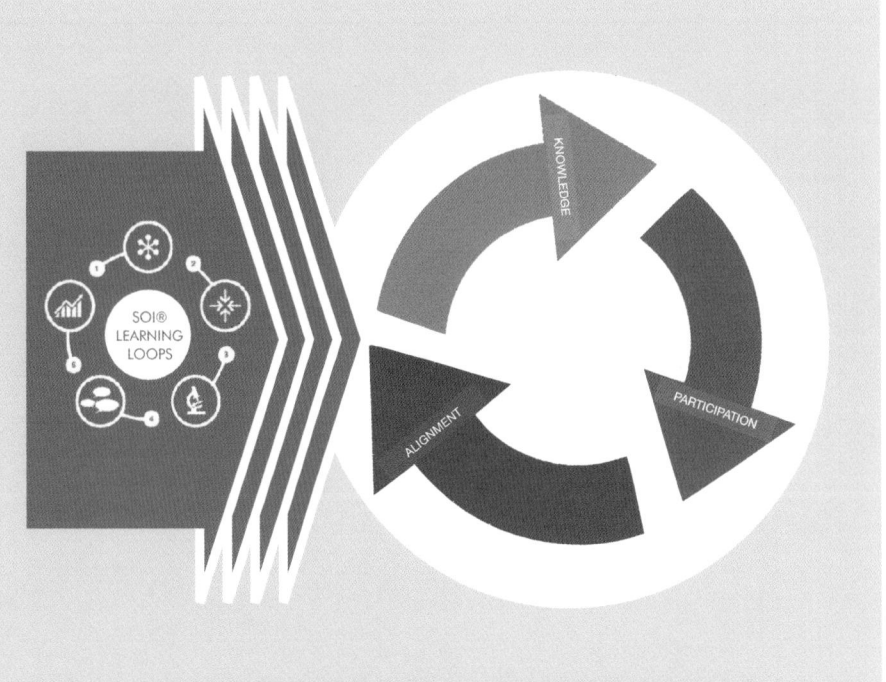

Proving it Your SOI® Learning Loops capture the performance of your business and the contribution it is making to the world in real time. Sharing knowledge encourages stakeholder participation and alignment that result in tangible outcomes that can be measured, validated and reported.

Making it happen

The technique for gaining this level of understanding and engagement comes from Constituent Voice™, a proven methodology developed by the social impact measurement pioneers at Keystone Accountability. Constituent Voice™ involves a simple-to-use five-step process that has inspired the SOI® Learning Loop cycle described below and illustrated on the following page.

Step One: Design

First up, decide what you want to measure, which means coming up with the right questions to ask your stakeholders. The following section sets questions you can ask your internal and external stakeholders. These questions are designed to tell you about two aspects of your SOI®:

- **Performance** – whether the key elements of your SOI® are being lived.

- **Impact** – whether people see how your SOI® delivers value to both society and your business.

Step Two: Collect

You should run short surveys at key touch-points (remember that you identified touch-points during the 'Identify' phase of the SOI® process) and make them an 'enquiry' rather than an investigative 'inquiry' – there's a difference! Keep the survey as light as possible: it should not take more than a couple of minutes to complete. If you have 12 questions that you want to ask, that's fine, but rotate them through micros-surveys of 2 to 4 questions, administered over several touch-points. The idea is to create a regular pulse check, not to engage people in one-off, arduous research exercises that take forever to complete and create a mountain of data too big to do anything useful with.

We are all weary of surveys, so make sure that your survey participation request is informative and engaging. Introducing your surveys with interesting facts about your SOI®, or the way that society is partnering with your business in light of your SOI®, is one way of developing a positive connection and a two-way dialogue.

Don't be shy about sharing the challenges your business faces; people know you have them, so sharing them is not only being genuine but also respectful of your audience. This is also the time to make a clear and powerful promise to your stakeholders to (a) report back on the survey data, and (b) involve them in dialogues that build on your findings and help co-create improvement actions. This makes it clear the survey is not a one-way extractive process but rather a two-way collaboration to develop improvements and generate value for all.

Step Three: Analyse

Analyse your survey data. KISS applies: keep it simple and keep it straightforward! To achieve that, think about tailoring your data analyses to each distinct stakeholder group and the interactions they have with the different functions of your business. What are the important issues and opportunities revealed by the data for that group? To discover the most relevant and actionable talking points, look for how different subsets of the stakeholder group may experience your business and SOI® differently.

5.1 SOI® LEARNING LOOPS (cont.)

Common characteristics to regard in data analysis include ethnicity, gender, age, and length of relationship with the company. It is also powerful for stakeholders to realise how responses may vary from one stakeholder group to another. "Why do customers, suppliers and staff have such different answers to this question?" is a great opener for a discussion.

Step Four: Discuss
This is the make or break step in the SOI® Learning Loop cycle. You must report back on your survey findings to your most important stakeholder groups, and use those reporting back sessions as opportunities to interpret the data and co-create ways to improve.

We call these suggestions to improve 'alignment actions', because an effective SOI® aligns values, behaviours, actions and results. Learning loops are your tool to achieve this ongoing alignment.

Of course, it's not always practical to invite and involve all members of a stakeholder group to these sense-making and solution-

making sessions, so it's vital to communicate the results so that all group members may appreciate that this process has indirectly included them. There are many ways to do this from broadcasting through social media to targeted communications such as email campaigns. As noted earlier, important results from this shared learning step can be included and used to introduce future surveys.

Step Five: Correct
This step is self-evident, and restarts the SOI® learning loop cycle.

1. Make the changes identified as alignment actions
2. Monitor alignment actions with future micro-survey questions that ask if the agreed actions are making things better.

By highlighting these actions in your general communications about your SOI®, you amplify how you and your stakeholders are working together to realise your contribution for the good of all.

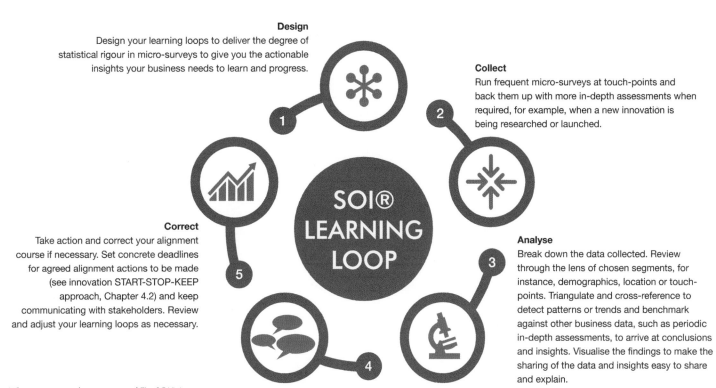

Design
Design your learning loops to deliver the degree of statistical rigour in micro-surveys to give you the actionable insights your business needs to learn and progress.

Collect
Run frequent micro-surveys at touch-points and back them up with more in-depth assessments when required, for example, when a new innovation is being researched or launched.

Correct
Take action and correct your alignment course if necessary. Set concrete deadlines for agreed alignment actions to be made (see innovation START-STOP-KEEP approach, Chapter 4.2) and keep communicating with stakeholders. Review and adjust your learning loops as necessary.

SOI® LEARNING LOOP

1
2
3
4
5

Analyse
Break down the data collected. Review through the lens of chosen segments, for instance, demographics, location or touch-points. Triangulate and cross-reference to detect patterns or trends and benchmark against other business data, such as periodic in-depth assessments, to arrive at conclusions and insights. Visualise the findings to make the sharing of the data and insights easy to share and explain.

Discuss
Engage stakeholders. Validate the data and encourage dialogue and collaboration to arrange further targeted investigations if required (see step 2, in-depth assessments). Discuss and agree actions for improved alignment.

What goes around comes around The SOI® Learning Loop is a simple five-step feedback cycle that will enable your business to build momentum and progress by regularly engaging with your various stakeholder groups.

Inspired by the Constituent Voice™ Action Cycle

5.2 INTERNAL PERFORMANCE METRICS

Below is a list of numbered propositions that can help you gather an **internal** view from your staff learning loop about the performance of your business and the degree of alignment you've achieved with your SOI®. I explain how to gather **external** views from your ecosystem on page 95.

1.0 Focus

1.1 My business has a sustainable call to action (SOI®) at the core that drives the entire organization.

1.2 Our SOI® has a clear results path that shows how our actions lead to positive contributions to society.

1.3 My business has set long and short-term goals to ensure it achieves alignment with its SOI®.

1.4 My business has clearly defined values that underpin the SOI®.

1.5 My business has a positioning statement that clearly explains the benefits of the SOI®.

2.0 Leadership

2.1 Leaders in my business actively promote the benefits of the SOI® consistently and clearly internally and externally.

2.2 Leaders in my business demonstrate the SOI® and values through their own individual actions.

2.3 Leaders in my business spend planned time with staff talking about the SOI® and the successes of the strategy and its future potential.

3.0 Communications

3.1 My business clearly communicates its objective and value to stakeholders.

3.2 My business encourages stakeholders to engage in its societal objective.

3.3 Our stakeholders are actively participating and interacting with our communication efforts.

3.4 My business achieves the levels of third-party advocacy required to support its objectives.

4.0 Products & services

4.1 My business delivers stakeholder experiences that clearly demonstrate our SOI®.

4.2 My business delivers products and services across the board that are fit for a sustainable future.

5.0 Processes & Systems

5.1 The functions of my business all have objectives that are aligned with the SOI®.

5.2 The SOI® and values inform sustainable procurement, HR, IT, and operational policies.

5.3 My business invests in technology aligned with the SOI® to deliver sustainable outcomes.

6.0 Innovation

6.1 My business is helping to change status quo thinking in its industry sector.

6.2 My business uses its SOI® to constantly innovate.

6.3 My business gathers feedback from its ecosystem to learn and improve.

6.4 My business regularly taps into the collective intelligence of its staff to refine or develop new ideas.

7.0 People & culture

7.1 My colleagues and I get the support we need to realise the SOI® and its values.

7.2 My business has performance indicators that detect staff actions and behaviours that align with the SOI®.

7.3 My business rewards staff actions and behaviours that align with the SOI®.

7.4 My business does not tolerate actions or behaviours that do not align with its values.

7.5 My business regularly celebrates successes related to the core objective.

Here and now, not then and there Your SOI® led business is a living organism, not a machine. This micro-survey turns propositions into questions so you can tap into what people are thinking and feeling here and now.

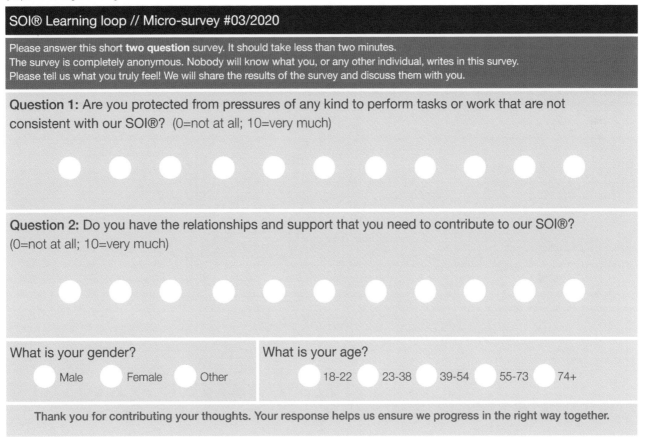

SOI® Learning loop // Micro-survey #03/2020

Please answer this short **two question** survey. It should take less than two minutes.
The survey is completely anonymous. Nobody will know what you, or any other individual, writes in this survey.
Please tell us what you truly feel! We will share the results of the survey and discuss them with you.

Question 1: Are you protected from pressures of any kind to perform tasks or work that are not consistent with our SOI®? (0=not at all; 10=very much)

Question 2: Do you have the relationships and support that you need to contribute to our SOI®? (0=not at all; 10=very much)

What is your gender?
○ Male ○ Female ○ Other

What is your age?
○ 18-22 ○ 23-38 ○ 39-54 ○ 55-73 ○ 74+

Thank you for contributing your thoughts. Your response helps us ensure we progress in the right way together.

5.3 INTERNAL IMPACT METRICS

Alignment with an SOI® will deliver positive short, medium and long-term impacts on your business and the stakeholders that surround it. You will see and experience the short and medium-term impacts of alignment with your SOI®, but the long-term impacts may only emerge after some years. Remember, your business is part of an ecosystem in which you and your business are playing an important but shared role.

Having a positive impact is what SOI® is all about, and understanding where it is happening is gained by posing two types of impact-focused enquiries through your system of SOI® Learning Loops that tap into the ecosystem.

The first enquiry asks stakeholders what changes they are seeing as a result of your SOI®. The second sizes up the quality of relationships that underlie your contributions to society.

Only open relationships of trust and mutual respect achieve success, so taking a regular pulse check to see how those relationships are doing is vitally important.

As with the performance metrics propositions, the stakeholder survey request is to rank two impact questions: The degree of 'perceived change' and the 'quality of relationships' on a scale of 1 to 10 (0 = not at all, 10 = very much). These questions are directed at staff to gain the internal view; the list for external stakeholders is on page 95.

1.0 Perceived change
1.1 Are there positive changes as a result of the SOI®?
1.2 Are these unintended as a result of the SOI®?
1.3 Is the SOI® contributing to a high performance culture in the business?
1.4 Are the values and SOI® are contributing to an inclusive culture at the business?
1.5 Do staff believe in and work to realise alignment with the SOI® and values?

2.0 Quality of relationships
2.1 Is it worth your effort to engage in the SOI® to make it more effective?
2.2 How much does the SOI® try to address what is important to you?
2.3 Can you hold leaders accountable for your SOI®?
2.4 To what extent does the SOI® foster better collaboration and cohesion in your business ecosystem?
2.5 Do business leaders act on the feedback about the SOI® that you and others give them?
2.6 Do you feel safe advancing your business's contributions to society at the expense of short-term profits?
2.7 Do you feel encouraged and supported to adapt SOI® plans and activities based on new evidence and learning?
2.8 To what extent do you have the relationships and connections you need to contribute to the SOI®?
2.9 Does the business help build an ecosystem of collaboration with external stakeholders?

You will want to probe for other factors that drive impact and you can do this through periodic in-depth assessments; but remember, micro-surveys are focused, short, frequent and quick.

Keeping it real The regular drumbeat of SOI® communications, micro-surveys, and well-publicised alignment actions will ensure that your SOI® is authentic and impactful. Annual surveys are for show. Frequent, touch-point based surveys will drive real action and outcomes across your business.

5.4 EXTERNAL LEARNING LOOPS

The exact same guidelines for operating an internal learning loop apply to learning loops that engage your external stakeholders. However, the propositions and questions are different.

1.0 Performance metrics
Your long list of propositions exploring performance from your internal staff learning loop can be shortened and simplified for external stakeholders.

(Likert scale 0 = not at all, 10 = very much)
1.1 [Your business name] has a positioning statement that clearly explains the benefits of the SOI®.
1.2 [your business name] has a sustainable core strategic objective (SOI®) that drives the company.
1.3 [your business name] has clearly defined values that underpin the SOI®.
1.4 My experience of [your business name] includes its SOI®.
1.5 [your business name] is helping to change status quo thinking in its industry sector.
1.6 [your business name] staff talk with me about the SOI®.
1.7 [your business name] invite me to engage in its public good objectives.
1.8 [your business name] achieves the levels of third-party advocacy required to support its objectives.
1.9 [your business name] delivers products and services across the board that are fit for a sustainable future.

2.0 Impact metrics
The internal impact-focused questions of two types – perceived change and relationship quality – give us more than we need for external stakeholders, so the task here is to again simplify. Pairing open questions seeking examples with closed Likert scale questions provides gold dust.

Perceived change
(Open questions)
2.1 What positive changes do you see as a result of [your business name]'s SOI®?
2.2 What unintended and/or negative changes do you see as a result of your SOI®?

Quality of relationships
(Likert scale 0 = not at all, 10 = very much)
2.3 How much does the SOI® try to address what is important to you?
2.4 Is it worth your effort to engage on the SOI® to make it more effective?
2.5 Can you hold leaders accountable for your SOI®?
2.6 Do leaders at [Your business name] act on the feedback about the SOI® that you and others give them?
2.7 Do you feel safe advancing your business's contributions to society at the expense of short-term profits?
2.8 Do you feel encouraged and supported to adapt SOI® plans and activities based on new evidence and learning?
2.9 To what extent do you have the relationships and connections you need to contribute to the SOI®?
2.10 To what extent does [Your business name] help build an ecosystem of collaboration with you and other stakeholders?

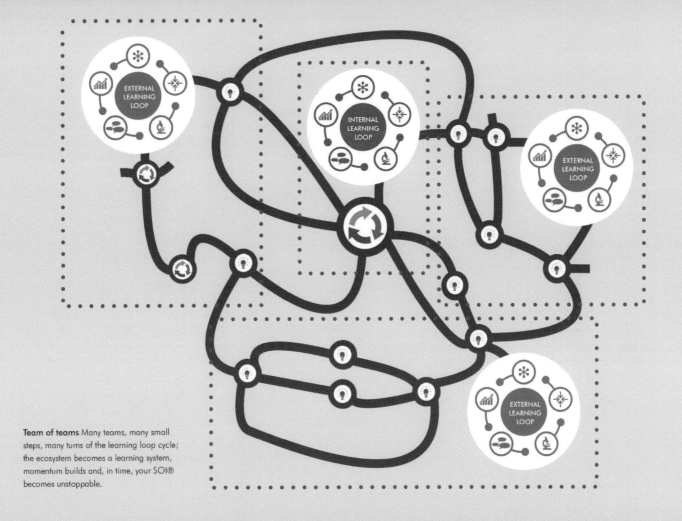

Team of teams Many teams, many small steps, many turns of the learning loop cycle; the ecosystem becomes a learning system, momentum builds and, in time, your SOI® becomes unstoppable.

5.5 LEARNING TO THRIVE

Having data that categorically demonstrates the value of your SOI® is especially important now, when there's so much scepticism about companies that signal but don't live their purpose – the emperors. Putting SOI® Learning Loops into action will enable you to prove your impact. For example, if you look at the fictional 'Feel-good' example I used in the define chapter, that company would be able to demonstrate outcomes like these:

• 72% of customers answer surveys with specific examples of how we help them 'feel-good'.

• When we launched our SOI®, staff often felt there was conflict between 'business as usual' and the goals and values of our 'feel-good' goal. Today, staff report overwhelmingly that they are 'protected from pressures of any kind to perform tasks or work that is not consistent with our SOI®'.

Progress like that does not happen as a result of top-down direction from above. It happens through a system of learning loops that frequently engage multiple stakeholders.

Ecosystem

When you have an SOI® Learning Loops system in place there is a realisation of a greater cause; that you're not working for a company in isolation but for an entire, interdependent ecosystem. Because your SOI® is designed to benefit your business, society in general and your diverse constituents in particular, your SOI® Learning Loops system makes the ecosystem around your company the unit of analysis and action, rather than the company alone. The performance and impact of your SOI® is measured with and for all your stakeholders. By participating in your SOI® Learning Loops, your stakeholders contribute to the good of all.

Simplicity

Meaningful solutions to the kinds of persistent societal problems that you are tackling with your SOI® are anything but simple to achieve. They are so complex, in fact, that it is counter-productive to try to measure the ultimate impacts. Instead, measuring simple-to-get signals and following up on them will deliver or support small, continual improvements aligned with your SOI®.

Momentum

Simplicity is the gateway to momentum. Only a light process can move through the cycle of steps quickly enough to create a drumbeat we can all follow, and which builds momentum. There is no set number of micro-surveys you should aim to run; that really depends on your capacity. You can't do everything, nor can you respond to every suggestion, so it's important that you balance the number of surveys with your ability to take action. Not delivering on promises is a shortcut to disappointment and frustration. Practice makes perfect and you will find the cycle of knowledge, participation and alignment will settle at a natural level that fits within your means. Over time this level will rise and momentum will increase.

Measuring is the final piece. Putting in place your SOI® Learning Loops system completes the playbook tasks required to pivot your business so that it is fit for a future which benefits all.

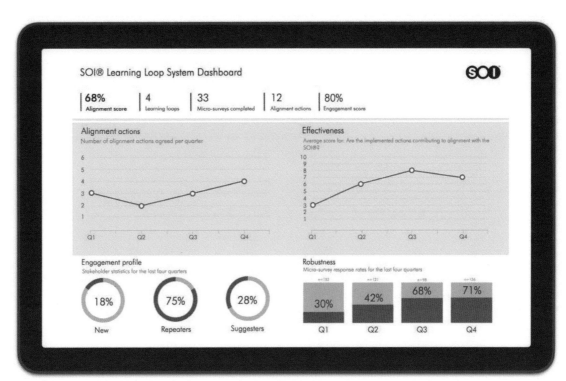

At a glance Your dashboard illustrates how well your learning system is working.

KEY POINTS

 Measuring your SOI® together with your stakeholders makes living proof that your SOI is authentic for them. It lets them know that they are the ones who get to say whether your SOI® is making an impact.

 You measure to improve and get better at contributing for the good of all. Your learning loop system generates actions to improve. Stakeholders decide whether implemented changes are steps in the right direction.

 Your most important performance indicator is alignment. If your staff are responding to surveys saying that they are experiencing pressures to work in ways that are not consistent with your SOI®, you can be sure there is important work to do with senior management.

 You gain momentum behind your SOI® through frequent cycles of stakeholder engagement that clearly demonstrate you are making progress in transforming your company.

 Learning loops hardwire you into the ecosystem around your business so that you avoid the trap of just ticking CSR and ESG boxes.

YOUR NOTES

SINGLE

ORGANIZING

IDEA

6.0

101-113

APPENDIX

Gain more from SOI® Learn about ongoing
support, how to get involved and a special bonus.

6.1 AFTERWORD

If there is such a fruitful opportunity for businesses to build thriving futures, why aren't more doing so? That's the question I sought to answer after the publication of my first book. Funded from the work I do for my clients and with the help of collaborators in my own ecosystem, I invited top business executives, business school professors, and leaders in sustainability, development and human rights to a series of dinner debates around the world. There were 15 events in all. The outcome of those debates drove me to write this Playbook and explain, in as much detail as possible, exactly how to change a business for good. Inevitably it's not enough, and the writing of it has led me to think about what more we can all do together to help move the needle.

Reporting

Emperors (see page 3) like to use their social do-gooding to tell stories that they believe will enhance their reputation, or at least protect it. This is misguided. Stories are fine and they may make people feel good, but they don't earn the kind of confidence investors, customers and employees are looking for. For that you need hard data-based evidence that your strategy is working; that it's making a difference to your and society's bottom lines, and will do so over the long term. Your SOI® Learning Loop system provides the mechanism for making the evidence-based case, and we have also developed additional assessment tools to help you measure and communicate how your SOI® creates value for all. To learn more about this topic, I suggest you look up the Sustainability Accounting Standards Board (SASB) and the measurement pioneers at Social Value International.

Start talking

Getting the conversation started is a hurdle in itself. Many of the people I've spoken to just say it's hard to even get the conversation going. People are too busy in the business to be working on the business. Don't give up. Here are three ways to tackle the time-poor:

"I've just got half a day"
SOI® SparkLabs
A highly interactive laboratory of exercises, challenges, discussions, analysis and synthesis of needs to take back into your enterprise to catalyse lasting change.

"I've just got an hour"
Change of Fortune - Interactive game
If your business is maxed out on workshops, how about a fun game that can be completed over a lunch hour? Look across and you will see it's free with this book.

"I've just got just 5 minutes"
Scorecard report
Complete a few questions and get a score and a personalised report.

All of the above can be found on our website along with templates for the tools described in this book, video explanations and ongoing support. Go to: www.singleorganizingidea.org

"I've got the time and expertise to help"
Talk to us
If you are an inspiring individual and are interested in learning how to help businesses thrive in the future, contact us here:
info@singleorganizingidea.org

SPECIAL BONUS

If you would like a copy of the fictional story from my award shortlisted book *CORE: How a Single Organizing Idea Can Change Business for Good* all you need to do is send an e-mail here:

bonus@singleorganizingidea.org

I will also send you the **interactive learning game** that goes with the story. If you want to get the conversation going and engage colleagues or friends in the need for businesses to change it's a great way to get things going. It comes with game instructions, character profiles and the story. As an extra bonus, I will give you a discount code for the entire book.

"The fictionalised story really grabbed me. It dramatically brings home the new reality of extreme global connectivity."
Prof David Grayson CBE, Emeritus Professor of Corporate Responsibility, Cranfield School of Management and author of *All In: The Future of Business Leadership*

6.2 GLOSSARY

Accountability
A term encompassing the evolving ways that companies are held to account by stakeholders. Today accountability norms go far beyond financial accounting standards and include stakeholder views on a company's effects on people and planet.

Circular Ecosystem/Circular Solutions
The circular concept redefines growth, re-focusing the definition of success on decoupling economic activity from the consumption of finite resources, and designing waste out of the system. It values economic, natural, and social capital, and is associated often with renewable energy sources.

Corporate Social Responsibility (CSR)
A general term covering the very broad spectrum of ways that businesses address their social and environmental responsibilities that range from tokenism and cosmetic to effective and fully integrated.

Customer Relationship Management (CRM)
Systematic practices and tools to manage interactions with customers and potential customers. A CRM system helps organizations manage customer relationships and streamline business processes to increase sales, improve customer service, increase profitability, and benefit society.

Ecosystem
James F. Moore introduced ecosystem the concept and defined it thus: "An economic community supported by a foundation of interacting organizations and individuals – the organisms of the business world. The economic community produces goods and services of value to customers, who are themselves members of the ecosystem. The member organisms also include suppliers, lead producers, competitors, and other stakeholders. Over time, they coevolve their capabilities and roles, and

tend to align themselves with the directions set by one or more central companies. Those companies holding leadership roles may change over time, but the function of ecosystem leader is valued by the community because it enables members to move toward shared visions to align their investments, and to find mutually supportive roles."

Enterprise Risk Management (ERM)
A plan-based business strategy that aims to identify, assess and prepare for any dangers, hazards, and other potentials for disaster — both physical and figurative – that may interfere with an organization's operations and objectives.

Environmental, Social, and Governance (ESG)
A set of concerns about company operations that investors use to evaluate potential investments. While once confined to socially conscious investors, ESG has become a mainstream norm. Diversity, equity and inclusion (DEI) considerations are now also entering investor assessments.

Index of Industrial Production (IIP)
A monthly economic indicator measuring real output in manufacturing, mining, electric and gas industries, relative to a base year.

International Organization for Standardization (ISO)
An independent, non-governmental, international organization that develops standards to ensure the quality, safety and efficiency of products, services and systems.

Kaizen
A Japanese business philosophy of continuous improvement. It prescribes improvement processes that involve all employees. Kaizen sees improvement in productivity as a gradual and methodical process.

Key Performance Indicators (KPIs)
Indicators used to monitor progress towards intended results. KPIs are utilised to keep focus on operational and strategic improvement.

Networked (or flat) Business Model
A business with a flat management structure is delayered in order to better integrate siloed internal resources, maximise collaboration and promote self-realisation, shared purpose, knowledge and information.

Purpose Washing
Like the term 'greenwashing', purpose washing is where brands and companies claim commitment to a specific cause without adopting this into their work or actions.

Silos
A function or part of a company that does not communicate or collaborate well with other parts of the company.

Small and Medium-sized Enterprises (SMEs)
A SME is generally a small or medium-sized enterprise with fewer than 250 employees. The EU also defines an SME as a business with fewer than 250 employees, a turnover of less than €50 million, or a balance sheet total of less than €43 million.

Societal Impact Analysis
The processes of analysing, monitoring and managing the intended and unintended social consequences, both positive and negative, of planned interventions (policies, programs, plans, projects) and any social change processes invoked by those interventions. Its primary purpose is to bring about a more sustainable and equitable biophysical and human environment.

Sustainable Development Goals (SDGs)
The Sustainable Development Goals (SDGs), also known as the Global Goals, were adopted by all United Nations Member States in 2015 as a universal call to action to end poverty, protect the planet, and ensure that all people enjoy peace and prosperity by 2030.

Sustainable Prosperity
The concept of equitable, long-term economic activity that meets the needs of the population fairly, and without the unviable use of natural resources.

Touchpoint
A point of contact or interaction between a business and its external stakeholders, especially customers. Sometimes referred to as a 'moment of truth'.

Traditional Business Model
Traditional businesses have a top-down chain of command with a sole leader at the top and subordinates at various levels below them. The hierarchical organization is designed to maximise profits for owners.

Triangulate
Interpreting and validating data by comparing it to other sources explaining the same phenomenon.

6.3 BIBLIOGRAPHY

Balmer, J. (2006). *The Nature and Management of Ethical Corporate Identity: Discussion Paper on Corporate Identity, Corporate Social Responsibility and Ethics.* The Braybrooke Press Ltd.

Browne, J. (2011). *Beyond Business.* Phoenix: Orion Books.

Browne, J. (2015). *Connect: How Companies Succeed by Radically Engaging with Society.* Penguin Random House.

Branson, R. (2013). *Screw Business as Usual.* Virgin Books.

Collier, P. (2019) *The Future of Capitalism.* Penguin Random House.

Collins, J. (2001). *Good to Great.* Random House Business.

Drucker, P. (2007). *Essential Drucker: Classic Drucker Collection.* Routledge.

Elkington, J. (2020) *Green Swans: The Coming Boom in Regenerative Capitalism.* Fast Company Press.

Elkington, J., & Hailes, J. (1989). *The Green Consumer Guide: From Shampoo to Champagne, How to Buy Goods That Don't Cost the Earth.* Guild Publishing.

Extinction Rebellion. (2019) *This is not a Drill.* Penguin.

Freedman, L. (2013). *Strategy, A History.* Oxford University Press.

Gaught, N. (2018) *Core: How a Single Organizing Idea Can Change Business for Good.* Routledge.

Gladwell, M. (2000). *Tipping Point: How Little Things can make a Big Difference.* Abacus.

Gino, F. (2013). *Sidetracked: Why our Decisions get Derailed, and how we can stick to the Plan.* Harvard Business Review Press.

Gnärig, B. (2015). *The Hedgehog and the Beetle: Disruption and Innovation in the Civil Society Sector.* International Civil Society Centre.

Ghemawat, P. (1991). *Commitment: The Dynamic of Strategy.* Macmillan.

Goleman, D. (1996). *Emotional Intelligence: Why it can Matter More Than IQ.* Bloomsbury.

Gosden, R. (1995). *Greening all the way to the bank.* Arena, 16, 35-37.

Gore, A. (2014). *The Future.* WH Allen.

Grafton, L. (2011). *The Shift: The Future of Work is Already Here.* William Collins.

Grafton, L. (2014). *The Key: How Corporations Succeed by Solving the World's Toughest Problems.* McGraw Hill Education.

Grayson, D. Coulter, C & Lee, M (2018) *All In: The Future of Business Leadership.* Routledge.

Hamel, G. (2012). *What Matters Now. How to Win in a World of Relentless Change, Ferocious Competition, and Unstoppable Innovation.* John Wiley & Sons.

Hamel, G. (2007). *The Future of Management.* Harvard Business School Press.

Hamel, G. & Zanini, M. (2020). *Humanocracy: Creating Organizations as Amazing as the People Inside Them.* Harvard Business Review Press.

Harari, Y.N. (2015). *Sapiens: A Brief History of Humankind.* Vintage.

Handy, C. (1995). *The Empty Raincoat: Making Sense of the Future.* Random House Business.

Handy, C. (2015). *The Second Curve: Thoughts on Reinventing Society.* Penguin Random House.

Handy, C. (2019) *21 Letters on Life and Its Challenges.* Hutchinson

Hersey, P. (1984) *The Situational Leader.* Warner Books.

Hodgkinson, G., & Starbuck, W. (2012). *The Oxford Handbook of Organizational Decision Making.* Oxford University Press.

Hendersen, R. (2020) *Reimagining Capitalism in a World on Fire*. Hatchette USA.

Khanna, P. (2016). *Connectography: Mapping the Future of Global Civilization*. Random House Trade.

Klein, N. (1999). *No Logo*. Harper Collins.

Klein, N. (2015). *This Changes Everything*. Penguin Random House.

Laloux, L. (2014) *Reinventing Organizations: A Guide to Creating Organizations Inspired by the Next Stage of Human Consciousness*. Nelson Parker.

Leadbeater, C. (2009). *We-Think: Mass Innovation, not Mass Production*. Profile Books.

Mayer, C. (2013). *Firm Commitment: Why the Corporation is Failing us and how to Restore Trust in it*. Oxford University Press.

Mayer, C. (2018). *Prosperity: Better Business Makes the Greater Good*. Oxford University Press.

Mehta, P. K. & Shenoy, S. (2011) *Infinite Vision*. Berrett Koehler Publishers

Mulgan, G. (2013). *The Locust and the Bee: Predators and Creators in Capitalism's Future*. Princeton University Press.

Murray, K. (2013). *The Language of Leaders: How Top CEOs Communicate to Inspire, Influence and Achieve Results*. Kogan Press.

O'Brien, J & Cave, A. (2017) *The Power of Purpose*. Pearson

Olins, W. (2014). *Brand New. The Shape of Brands to Come*. Thames & Hudson.

Peters, S. (2012). *The Chimp Paradox, The Mind Management Programme for Confidence, Success and Happiness*. Vermillion.

Robertson, B.J. (2015) *Holacracy: The Revolutionary Management System That Abolishes Hierarchy*. Portfolio Penguin.

Roddick, A. (2000). *Business as Unusual, My Entrepreneurial Journey, Profits with Principles*. Harper Collins.

Raworth, K. (2017). *Doughnut Economics, Seven Ways to Think Like a 21st-Century Economist*. Penguin Random House.

Schien, E. (2010). *Organizational Culture and Leadership - 4th Edition*. Jossey-Bass.

Sinek, S. *Start With Why: How Great Leaders Inspire Everyone To Take Action*. Penguin.

Smith, S. & Milligan, A. (2015) *On Purpose: Delivering a Branded Customer Experience People Love*. Kogan Page.

Steiber, A. (2013). *The Google Model: Managing Continuous Innovation in a Rapidly Changing World*. Springer Cham Heidelberg.

Surowiecki, J. (2005). *The Wisdom of Crowds: Why the Many Are Smarter Than the Few*. Abacus.

Taleb, N. N. (2008) *The Black Swan: The Impact of the Highly Improbable*. Penguin.

Taleb, N. N. (2018) *Skin in the Game: Hidden Asymmetries in Daily Life*. Allen Lane.

Thunberg, G. (2019). *No One is too Small to Make a Difference*. Penguin Random House.

Yunas, M. (2010). *Building Social Business: The New Kind of Capitalism that Serves Humanity's Most Pressing Needs*. Public Affairs Books.

6.4 ACKNOWLEDGEMENTS

This book is the result of generosity, wisdom and collaboration. As soon as my first book *CORE: How a Single Organizing Idea Can Change Business for Good* was published I embarked on a self-funded (and carbon offset) book tour, inviting business leaders, thought leaders, academics, sustainability experts, human rights, governmental and non-governmental people to business roundtables to discuss the challenges we are facing, and more importantly, how we get businesses to change and help. Named the 'Core Dinner Debates', there were 15 events in all. I learnt a great deal, but by far the most important lesson was that evidence and protest don't change things on their own. To make real change happen people need tools. That's when I decided to write *CORE: The Playbook* and share the entire SOI® process and tools. I can't name every single person who attended the debates but I am pleased to be able to thank and acknowledge the organizations they came from. **Business:** Arla Foods International, Aviva, Bank of New Zealand, Banque Libano-Française, Blackrock, Blom Bank, Cedenco Foods, Centrica, Community Clothing, Coop Danmark, Decathlon Canada, Dell, Dig Inn, Douglas Pharmaceuticals, Fonterra, Fiera Capital, FransaBank, Gaz Métro (Canada), Hawkins, HP, IBM (Blockchain), Inter Ikea Group, IPSOS MORI, Kordia, KPMG, Leon, Lyft, Maersk, Marks & Spencers, MasterCard, Nordic Impact, Novo Nordisk, NTD Apparel, Ørsted, Portland Trust, Pearson, Ripple, Société Générale, SourceTrace, Sumitomo, Unilever, Visa, Walmart, **Academia:** American University of Beirut, Cambridge University (CISL), Copenhagen Business School, Cranfield Business School, John Hopkins, Metropolitan University, London Säid Business School, Oxford, Harvard (Shared Value Initiative), Questrom School of Business - Boston University, **NGOs** ABET, Ashoka, B Corps (UK), Business Fights Poverty, CARE, Circular Norway, Clinton Foundation, Conference Board of Canada, DAI, Danish Institute for Human Rights, DEVEX, Ethical Trading Initiative, Forum for the Future, InterAction, InterAmerican Development Bank, International Rescue Committee, Investment Fund for Developing Countries, Global Communities, Global Partnership for Sustainable Development Data, Nesta, Oxfam, Save the Children, Sustainable Brands, Sustainatopia, The Sustainability Curriculum Consortium, The World Bank, UNDP, UN New York, UN Global Compact (Lebanon), US Chamber of Commerce Foundation, US Green Building Council, Vital Voices, World Cocoa Foundation, WWF, **Government:** New Zealand Trade & Enterprise, Ministry of Foreign Affairs of Denmark.

Contributors

I could not have possibly completed this book without the generosity, knowledge and energy of my Single Organizing Idea Ltd partners. I am honoured to call them my friends and to be working hard with them to bring SOI® thinking to an ever- increasing audience of business leaders asking for practical tools they can use to contribute to a more sustainable future through their enterprise.

Nick Davies, Founder Neighbourly

Nick is an ex-agency marketer with 30 years experience helping some of the world's best-known companies promote their products. But his world view was changed by the 2009 recession, and a realisation that companies must pursue societal and economic return in equal measure if they are to remain relevant and achieve sustainable success.

Nick launched Neighbourly.com in July 2014 to help companies like Marks and Spencer, Danone, Coca-Cola and Samsung find the right balance between value for shareholders and value for society. These companies and many others engaged Neighbourly to manage their volunteering and donated funds, and surplus products at huge scale, all through a single, game-changing, social platform.

By making contribution simple, collaborative and fun, Neighbourly aligns the interests of business and society to create a powerful force for good in the world. Neighbourly is a founding UK B-Corporation and winner of numerous awards, including Unilever Foundry 50 (2015), Bloomberg Business Innovators (2016) and FT ArcelorMittal Boldness in Business (2019).

David Bonbright, Co-founder & CEO
Keystone Accountability

As a professional grant-maker and manager with some of the world's leading foundations, David Bonbright sought innovative approaches to strengthening citizen self-organization in place of prevailing bureaucratic, top-down models. While with the Ford Foundation, David was declared persona non grata by the apartheid government in South Africa for helping fund the liberation struggle. In the early 1990s, in the final years of that struggle, he catalysed the development of key building block organizations for civil society in the new South Africa.

During that time, he had an unexpected invitation to meet with Nelson Mandela, who reinforced that governments, businesses and nonprofits all run aground when they fail to listen to those they intend to help, and that "in social change, as in our personal and social lives, it is relationships that determine outcomes". Inspired by his experiences, he founded and now runs an international nonprofit organization dedicated to bringing constituent feedback to social change practice through his widely praised performance measurement method Constituent Voice.

Ian Mitchell, CEO BGI Group
Ian grew up in an entrepreneurial family with business being part of the fabric of daily life. After completing his MSc in International Development, Administration and Planning, Ian worked for the International Development Agency in Kenya and The Body Shop Fair Trade Department before turning his hand to the telecommunications industry.

Ian went on to co-found the telecoms business Direct Response in a garage in East London. The business grew into a group employing over 1,500 people across the UK, winning awards for growth, service excellence and the coveted Investors In People Gold Award. In 2018 the group was sold. Wishing to continue pursuing his passion for business and contribute his experiences to the progress of SMEs in particular, Ian became CEO of the London-based BGI Group. There, he leads a team dedicated to helping increase SMEs' holistic value.

6.5 ABOUT THE AUTHOR

Neil Gaught is an award-winning author, former soldier, designer, strategic advisor, self-styled business humaniser and speaker. He is what Malcolm Gladwell would call an outlier.

Neil was born in Hertfordshire but grew up on the Lancashire side of the Pennines. Following a short four-year spell in the British Army, a rather shorter one in the French Foreign Legion, some adventures in Africa, and a period of homelessness, he furthered his education at what is now the University of Arts, London, where he gained a BA(Hons) in Graphic Design.

A year after graduating in 1990 he founded an award-winning London-based design consultancy. Having successfully run the business for 10 years he sold it to an advertising agency before joining the world's largest communications, advertising and PR multinational, WPP. There he took a leading role on a variety of high-profile global branding projects for the likes of Merrill Lynch, DeBeers, BP, Arthur Andersen, Scottish Power, BG Group and Standard Chartered Bank, amongst others.

In 2003, frustrated with the corporate world of spin he was contributing to, and up for a new adventure, Neil and his young family moved to Auckland, New Zealand. Following a short spell with the leading design agency there, Neil re-established his independent status to pursue his own ideas and develop the thinking behind Single Organizing Idea (SOI®). Since returning to the UK in 2009, he has advised and helped positively change a wide variety of enterprises from business multinationals to international NGOs, billionaire-owned foundations to start-ups, faith-based organizations and government institutions across the world.

In 2018 his book CORE: How a Single Organizing Idea Can Change Business for Good was shortlisted for the Business Book of the Year Award. Drawing on stories, case studies and his own experiences working in the field across five continents, its pragmatic no-nonsense approach to taking on 'business as usual' has received wide recognition and significant praise from leading figures in business and sustainability, including John Elkington, Mike Barry, Charles Leadbetter and Charles Handy.

The perfect introduction to the **CORE Playbook**

CORE: How a Single Organizing Idea can Change Business for Good
Routledge 2018

Though the tides of change are engaging the minds of business leaders, most are still trapped behind their brands and an approach to CSR that is out of step with a connected society that increasingly question who these businesses really are and what drives their purpose.

Drawing on a story of our times, case studies, and front-line experiences, Gaught's no-nonsense approach sets aside ideals to confront the realities of business reform. It demonstrates the power and potential that a single idea, shaped and implemented to benefit all stakeholders, can bring to any business that is prepared to take its head out of the sand and proactively respond to the challenges being set by customers, employees, investors and the planet itself.

"Business should help people learn how they can live better lives and lead society to create the systems and technologies to do so. Core is a great guide to how business can take on that task."
Charles Leadbeater, author of *We Think*

"No business can prosper in the future without a clear purpose and here, at last, is a practical management tool to turn a great theory into gritty reality."
Mike Barry, Former Director, M&S Plan A

"Timely, engaging, valuable and practical."
Zahid Torres-Rahim, Founder, Business Fights Poverty

"The fictionalised story really grabbed me. It dramatically brings home the new reality of extreme global connectivity."
Prof David Grayson CBE, Emeritus Professor of Corporate Responsibility, Cranfield School of Management and author of *All In: The Future of Business Leadership*

"SOI® has so much more potential to make a difference than a simple purpose."
Charles Handy, Leading business management thinker and author of *The Second Curve: Thoughts on Reinventing Society*

www.singleorganizingidea.org

Printed in Great Britain
by Amazon

54063303R00069